T0128124

A CULT CHALLENGE TO THE CHURCH

Why Are People Looking
for a Relationship
with God in All
the Wrong Places?

WM. W. WELLS

WESTBOW
PRESS®
A DIVISION OF THOMAS NELSON
& ZONDERVAN

This book is a work of non-fiction. Unless otherwise noted, the author and the publisher make no explicit guarantees as to the accuracy of the information contained in this book and in some cases, names of people and places have been altered to protect their privacy.

WestBow Press books may be ordered through booksellers or by contacting:

WestBow Press
A Division of Thomas Nelson & Zondervan
1663 Liberty Drive
Bloomington, IN 47403
www.westbowpress.com
1 (866) 928-1240

Because of the dynamic nature of the Internet, any web addresses or links contained in this book may have changed since publication and may no longer be valid. The views expressed in this work are solely those of the author and do not necessarily reflect the views of the publisher, and the publisher hereby disclaims any responsibility for them.

Any people depicted in stock imagery provided by Getty Images are models, and such images are being used for illustrative purposes only. Certain stock imagery © Getty Images.

Unless otherwise indicated, all Scripture quotations are from the ESV® Bible (The Holy Bible, English Standard Version®), copyright © 2001 by Crossway, a publishing ministry of Good News Publishers. Used by permission. All rights reserved.

Scripture marked (KJV) taken from the King James Version of the Bible.

ISBN: 978-1-9736-9716-9 (sc)
ISBN: 978-1-9736-9715-2 (e)

Print information available on the last page.

WestBow Press rev. date: 07/28/2020

CONTENTS

CHAPTER ONE

INTRODUCTION

Moonie?

In 2016, I was at breakfast with a large group of Christian friends, including several pastors. We had just been to a prayer meeting held in the wooded area at a local nursery. My friend introduced me as "Moonie Bill." When he explained that I had been a Moonie at one time, several sat straight up. Immediately, one wide eyed pastor asked, "Why?" Since the "Moonies" have receded from public view in the last few decades, I may have to explain who they are before I go on to answer why.

I was a member of the Unification Church, formally known as the Holy Spirit Association for the Unification of World Christianity (HSA-UWC), but since, renamed Family Federation for World Peace and Unification (FFWPU), or simply Unificationism. The term Moonie is a slur coined by the press referring to a follower of the founder, leader, and self-proclaimed second coming of Christ, Sun Myung Moon. In the seventies and eighties, the Moonies were aggressively evangelizing and fundraising, selling flowers and candy on street corners and parking lots. They held massive rallies in most major American cities. They also had a large presence in Korea, where the movement was founded, and in Japan. The Moonies had established a significant presence in

England, Germany and France. They were hard to avoid. Most of the significant news magazines ran stories about Moon, usually negative.

The basic teachings of the church are contained in the book titled *Divine Principle*, which purports to explain the Bible and all of Biblical and subsequent history. Of course, it all leads up to the second coming of the Messiah in Korea, therefore, Sun Myung Moon. Reverend Moon, as he was referred to by the church, was continually giving talks to church members, which were published under the title "Master Speaks." As a church leader, I was present for many of these talks.

Programming

Conservative Christians considered the "Moonies" to be a cult and therefore a menace. News articles and books published all sorts of lurid stories about the church. The church was accused of brainwashing and mind control. Several professional "deprogrammers" began selling their services to distraught parents. It was claimed that members weren't allowed to leave the church and were held by some form of mind control, so the only way to get them out was to kidnap the members and "deprogram" them. However, since these self-styled "deprogrammers" themselves had no way to get members out of the church without resorted to brainwashing techniques, starting with kidnapping and confinement against the subject's will, sleep deprivation, and constant verbal bombardment, the parents were almost always involved, at least with the initial kidnapping. The presence of the parents was necessary to give protection from lawsuits or other legal ramifications.

Many members escaped their captors, some multiple times, and returned to the Unification Church. Very few were willing to bring charges against their captors since close family members were involved. The deprogrammers were shut down slowly. When charges were brought against them the deprogrammers often faced jail time. In one case which happened while I was at the seminary, one of the students was kidnapped by a well-known self-styled deprogrammer. By this time, larger church facilities, including the seminary, had security details. Our security staff had become aware of the presence of deprogrammers in the area, and knew where their "safe-house" was. They immediately called the police and headed to the house. They arrived at about the same time as the police. When the police arrived, the deprogrammer was pistol whipping the church member in the driveway. Needless to say, that deprogrammer found himself in jail.

I do not want to sound like an advocate for the Moonies, but the Moonies were not brainwashed ever. It is simply not possible to "brainwash" someone in any meaningful sense of the word without confinement. I am not aware of any situation in which the Moonies held someone against their will. Brainwashing involves intense mental and sometimes physical pressure. This is not possible to do on a large scale in a liberal democratic society. Moreover, as soon as a person walks out the door into the urban environment, all of your social interactions mitigate against a forced viewpoint. So, let me set the record straight, I was not brainwashed. I was not placed under any extraordinary mental or physical pressure. I was not held against my will. I am quite sure I was not fed any mind-altering substance. For sure, the "deprogrammers" were busy manufacturing these stories in order to bolster their argument for their extreme techniques. Because many people found it hard to understand why someone would join this "cult," all of these wild accusations soon found their way into print.

The answer to why I joined the Unification Church involves a much more complex journey. To begin with, I was not happy with the Christianity that I grew up in. When I arrived at university in 1970, the religious choices were staggering. I examined all of the major religions and lots of new startups. None of the other popular alternatives appealed to me (Zen Buddhism, Hare Krishna, Ananda Marga, Transcendental Meditation, Scientology and so on). The Unification Church offered a fresh approach to Christianity that appealed to the educated mind. Again, I am not advocating for the Unification Church or their theology. Instead, much of what I have to say has to do with how Christianity is failing the young and how this has provided the bad theology of the Unification Church and similar new religious movements an open door to enter. In many ways, this book is more about Christianity than about the Unification Church. Although I was raised a Christian, like many of my generation I lost all interest in Christianity, or more specifically, in the Church.

The Moonies had a very effective technique which they referred to as "love bombing." Essentially, it involved surrounding new recruits with a warm, welcoming, and safe environment. For young men and women who did not have strong social ties, this could prove to be more powerful than any other attraction. For young recruits, living was communal, 24/7. Moonies slept in what amounted to bunkhouses, men and women strictly separate. We ate together, prayed together, studied together and went to work in teams.

The most controversial practice of the Moonies was that Sun Myung Moon would personally match couples and perform mass weddings of thousands of couples at a time. He and Mrs. Moon called themselves the "True Parents," believing that their mission was to restore humanity to its condition before the fall of Adam and Eve into sin. I was matched with a French girl in 1979. Moon, himself, selected the two of us. We had a few minutes to talk and decide yes or no. We accepted. We were to have been a part of the mass wedding of 2075 couples in Madison Square Garden, which occurred on July 1, 1982. An even larger wedding of 30,000 couples was held in Washington DC in 1997.

What This Book Is About

To start with, this book is about why anyone raised Christian would want to join the Moonies or any other non-Christian religion, and what we (I say we, because I am now a Biblically centered Christian) can do about it. This is a book discussing the issues of an outsider contending with the Christian insider. I want to discuss Christians and how they present themselves to Moonies and to the rest of the world. The Moonies had, and probably still have, many excellent qualities, They prayed fervently, studied hard, and worked selflessly to the point of exhaustion. Moonies were contending with Christianity as a whole, calling the body of Christ back to being world-changers.

Secondly, this book is about goals. What is the goal of Christianity, outlined in scripture, as opposed to the actions of Christians in the world, and as opposed to new religious movements like the Moonies?

The following accounts are real events that happened during my time as a member of the Unification Church (1974-1982). There are stories of angry Christians cowed by cheerful Moonies. There is the Christian brother with whom I prayed who asked if he could pray again after he heard my "Moonie" prayer. There were the many who threw at me the few Bible quotes they knew, and then found themselves confounded by my understanding of the scriptures. There is even a pastor who in frustration burst out, "Jesus is not about love!"

In the end, my understanding of scriptures was seriously flawed. And, although I did cow a few Christians, I do not think it was because of my superior wisdom, but because of their lack of understanding of the gospel that they had been treasured with. It should never be the case that a Christian is left without an adequate response to a Mormon, or a Moonie, or a Muslim, or what have you. For the most part, this book is about situations in which I, as a Moonie, walked away from a Christian feeling that I had proven them wrong and myself right. In that sense, this could be considered an indictment of Christianity.

I would also like to explore some of the reasons by which someone grows up in the church, but ends up wanting little or nothing to do with the church. Many such persons still call themselves Christian, but have no real connection to any church at all. Some call themselves Christian but hate the church. And, some would rather call themselves a witch than a Christian.

Myself, I went through several stages: atheist, agnostic, pro-Christ but anti-Church, then heretical Christian. I am a committed Christian now. I am fairly certain that my theology is in keeping with sound Christian tradition. I realize that there are a lot of differences in what is considered the Truth. I am an active member of a local church. That church is active in bringing pastors and churches together, as well as making the church an important part of the community life. Therefore, I am hoping that everything contained herein will be helpful towards bringing health to the body of Christ.

Leaving

Another question that often comes up is, "How did you get out?" This refers to the impression left by books and articles, especially by the so-called "deprogrammers," who claimed the above-mentioned brainwashing and other tactics were used by the church to make it next to impossible to leave. The fact is that when I was ready to go, I packed my things and walked out. It was difficult, because I left behind my entire social network. Moreover, I was walking out into New York City, which embraces no one. I did not tell anyone I was leaving for there would have been a long line of friends trying to "reason" with me.

I left because I had become disillusioned with the Unification Church's ability to create a positive impact. In many ways, it was the same disillusion that I had with the Christianity of my youth. Most of all, I felt that I was in a situation where I myself wasn't doing anything useful. I was sacrificing everything. I was approaching my thirtieth birthday, didn't have a real job and I didn't own a thing but the clothes on my back, and I had a difficult time saying it was all worth it.

Perhaps more importantly, although I had been matched with a fiancé who had returned to France, I began a clandestine relationship with another girl, also a church member. This was strictly forbidden, as it should have been. Both of us had already decided that we had had enough of the Moonie life and left the church January 1, 1982. We got married shortly thereafter. I did not leave harboring ill feeling toward the Unification Church, but I am definitely no longer affiliated in any way with the Unification Church. I am a safely born-again Christian.

To my knowledge, the current organization formally known as the Family Federation for World Peace and Unification has changed considerably, particularly since the death of the founder Sun Myung Moon in 2012. The organization has gone through several succession struggles and the current organization is headed up by one of Moon's daughters. Two of Moon's sons have formed their own dissident offshoot, the Sanctuary Church, known for packing AR-15s.

My Moonie Experience

As I stated, I was a Moonie from 1974, when I graduated college, until January 1, 1982. I joined a team in Missoula, Montana, and after a short time was sent to Seattle and then on to New York City. I was occasionally assigned to fundraising teams, but was mostly assigned to street evangelizing teams. Because I had a college degree, I was selected as an anti-Communism educator in a satellite group called the Freedom Leadership Foundation. I worked out of the Chicago church center doing research and teaching.

In 1976, I was selected for Unification Theological Seminary. This was the second year of the seminary's existence, and it was considered an honor to be selected. Despite being a Moonie seminary, UTS provided a broad experience in contemporary mainline Christian teaching. Professors were from several established denominations, including Presbyterian, Dutch Reform, Catholic and Greek Orthodox, as well as a Rabbi. Many were still teaching at other seminaries. I distinguished myself as a rebel while at the seminary by delivering the first sermon which got a rebuttal. After that, I became the hero of every malcontent in the church. This was not really what I wanted, and their adulation was more disconcerting to me than the evil eye I got from those who were the self-appointed keepers of the faith.

After graduation, the entire class was sent to England for nine months. There, we street witnessed and ran crusades throughout the country. For a large part of the time, I rented a flat with non-church members. This gave me a great introduction to local English students.

After England, I was installed as the leader of the Wisconsin church, which was mainly one center in Milwaukee. The center was deep in debt, so my only real accomplishment there was to pay off the largest part of that debt. After a year of managing a small state center, I was happy to be called back to New York, where I worked with others in a program to develop teaching materials and other media for the church.

I left the church while I was in New York and began to work as a freelance theatrical designer and technician. My college degree was a Bachelor of Fine Arts in theatrical design. For more than a year, I would receive occasional visits from Moonie friends trying to convince me to come back to the fold. This did not please my wife. Although she had also been a Moonie, her profile wasn't as high. She did not receive visits from Moonie friends trying to coax her back to the fold. I am sure that she feared I would be pulled away by my friends.

Seminary gave a jolt to my abiding interest in understanding my place in the universe, to God and to all things Christian. I still enjoy reading theology. However, it wasn't until the late eighties when my small family and I moved to Texas that I decided to return to the church of my youth, the Presbyterians. Seminary had given me a broad exposure to several denominations, and I had become accepting of the inadequacies of the church in general and the Presbyterians in particular. Somehow, age and maturity softened my view of the church. In 1999, I joined a charismatic church, where I have grown tremendously in my commitment to Christ and my understanding of the gospel. I have continued to serve in that small non-denominational church and have learned to have grace toward the ways in which the church struggles to be the body of Christ. I am a strong proponent of churches reaching across denominational and cultural boundaries to work together and particularly to pray together for the Kingdom of God here on earth. I believe our Christianity is deeply enriched when we encounter and consider the vast history of Christianity and the many variations that encompass the body of Christ, and believe it or not, I can thank my education at Unification Theological Seminary for that.

In some ways, I could be accused of still following a Moonie path, as in many ways building the kingdom of God was, and to my understanding, still is the main goal of the Moonies. The problem for Moonies is essentially the problem of the fourth century heretic Pelagius: thinking that God's Kingdom can be established without dying to Jesus and accepting the Holy Spirit as our guide, our strength, and as our mentor. The king in the Kingdom is still Jesus.

Theology

In the course of this book I intend to introduce some of the theologians I met in seminary or others that subsequent study introduced me to. The reason is fairly simple, Christians struggle to act like Christians when their understanding of Christian history and of the gospel is weak. This is a problem particularly prominent in many of the churches in my charismatic circle. This is not an academic book, and so I want to keep my discussion easy to understand for all readers. Unfortunately, even well-trained theologians can get confused and come up with some wild ideas. When I was in seminary, the "Death of God" theology was prominent, even gaining a spot on the cover of Time magazine. Some of the theologians associated with that movement were frequent visitors to our seminary.

Liberation theology was also popular. Its embrace of Marxism put them at odds with Unificationism. However, I read several authors involved in Liberation theology and attended, along with a group of Moonies, a Paulo Freire seminar at a Maryknoll seminary. The Unificationist attitude towards those they disagreed with was to study their arguments in order to intelligently discuss them.

Moon started as a Christian, and hence had a theology that was heavily Christian in nature. I will be discussing the ways in which Moonie doctrines seriously undercut Christian teaching. Moon also embraced Korean folk traditions and felt that all religions are similar in their spiritual desires. It is fair to say that Moonie theology leans heavily in the direction of New Age spirituality.

CHAPTER TWO

WHEN DID GOD DIE?

Secular City

In 1965, Harvey Cox wrote *The Secular City*. As theology goes, it was an unqualified best seller from the first printing. It was a heady celebration of the end of religion as a meaningful component of life as we know it. Cox has been accused of being part of the "death of God" movement in theology, although Cox disliked that label and denied the charge.

In 1976, I entered seminary. That academic year, Cox made his first visit to speak to Unification Theological Seminary. He arrived with his young daughter. Some of us suspected he brought her to protect himself against any intense recruitment devices like those the Moonies were rumored by the press to employ. He had no need to worry. The seminary was delighted to have him and warmly welcomed him. He looked every bit the successful author, with a well-worn turtleneck and a salt and pepper beard. He clearly enjoyed his visit and happily returned the next year.

Cox's return visit included a bit of fun, as he was carried into the dining hall wearing a fools hat in honor of his 1969 book *The Feast of Fools*, celebrating festivity and fantasy. But, his book *The Secular City* is his most significant work by far.

By 1976, Cox's original thesis, that religion was coming to an end, had to have been wearing thin. Explo '72 packed 100,000 young people into the Cotton Bowl for several days of unabashed celebration of Christianity. New religious movements seemed to be popping up every day. In particular, Eastern religions were attracting large numbers of adherents. Ashrams and religious communes seemed to be everywhere. New religions, such as the Moonies, seemed to be exploding. In fact, Cox's first visit to the seminary was connected to research for his next book *Turning East*, published in 1977, which tracks the surprising rise of Eastern religion in the West. And yet, had you asked me about the significance of religion in 1965, when *The Secular City* was published and when I was poised to enter high school, I would have agreed with his earlier thesis; religion, as we know it, was ready to disappear. At that point, I was refusing to go to church with the family, having decided the entire exercise was stupid and a waste of time.

By 1976, things had changed considerably for me. I had graduated college with a Bachelor of Fine Arts in theater and joined an extremely controversial church, the Unification Church. In fact, I was at the Unification Theological Seminary to study for a Masters of Religious Education. For me, the intervening years had transformed the questions of God and religion from a dead issue to a very live one.

Never-the-less, for many people questions of God and religion ceased to play any part in their lives. These Death of God theologians had realized something significant. Despite a revival of religious interest, for a very large number of people here in America, the questions of religion and God were and are irrelevant. While polls show that just less than 40% of Americans attend church regularly, an article in Outreach Magazine quotes a 2005 study showing the actual numbers are less than half of that and declining (Barnes and Lowery 2018). A friend of mine has started an informal poll asking people, "which interests you more: Christianity or witchcraft?" The answers lean heavily in the direction of witchcraft, and we live in Texas, still considered part of the Bible belt. Millions of Americans who grew up in Christian homes want nothing to do with Christianity. For these people, the fires of hell seem like preacher babble. For them, God is either dead or is some vague force or power out there which has nothing to do with their lives. "God is watching us from a distance," croons one pop song refrain.

Why Talk About Theology

As a child, I was thinking about God. Whenever things were said about God, I had questions. When I didn't get answers or got obviously wrong or unhelpful answers, I started working on my own conclusions. My first conclusion was that my instructor didn't know what they were talking about. My favorite goofy answer was to my desire to have the Trinity explained, to which an eager Christian explained that the Trinity is just like Three-in-One oil. He was quite certain that his answer made things very clear.

I grew up in church. I was asking people who should have been able to give me some sort of an intelligent answer, or to at least steer me in the right direction. For an increasing number of people, they haven't grow up in church and may have never been in any sort of formal religious setting outside of a wedding or funeral. If they have questions, where do they get intelligent answers?

It seems that popular culture supplies many people their answers. God appears as an impersonal "Force" in the Star Wars movies. There is a "Dark Force" which stands in opposition. Several movies have portrayed life on this planet as having been placed here by an alien race. So maybe God, or the gods, are alien beings as in the movie *Stargate*? Erich von Däniken published the popular book *Chariots of the Gods* in 1968, which put forward the basic premises expolored in *Stargate* and other movies.

Pop culture has all sorts of quick and easy answers. Unfortunately, the questions are too serious for quick and easy answers. Pop culture answers create more confusion than intelligence. Theologians are well educated professionals who think about these difficult questions. Since my first encounters with men like Cox and Rubenstein, who we will talk about shortly, I have enjoyed reading what they have to say. Even when I disagree, I feel that they are drawing me closer to deep truths.

Theology and theologians can become entrapped in thoughts about God and religion that have nothing to do with practical Christianity. They can also leave the impression that having the right ideas about God is all that is required of a Christian. This is the opposite problem from those Christians that I grew up with who had become so busy doing Church, that they lost sight of the who, what and why. By looking at some theological insights, we may begin to understand some of the practical problems that I will be discussing in this book.

It was the theologians who first began to grapple with a world in which God no longer played a meaningful part. God has become irrelevant to the modern Western world. Many of us are no longer living in that world divorced from God. I include myself with those who see God at work on a daily basis. But for many of the people I meet, God and God talk is an immediate non-starter. Many, even practicing Christians, do not know basic Bible stories. I often talk to people who have never been to church and know little or nothing about Christianity or any other major religion. For most of them, they see themselves as functioning just fine without God, even if they do call themselves Christian.

Death of God

Nietzsche famously pronounced, "God is dead. God remains dead, and we have killed him." In the 1950's and 1960's, several theologians took up this idea, creating the Death of God theology. So, here is my question, if these theologians, the men who actually train the pastors who cultivate the faith of their congregations, cannot see that God is very much alive and with us, then why would we expect to see God in our churches? Nietzsche is also quoted as saying of the Church, "His disciples should look more redeemed."

By the time I entered high school, church seemed to be the last place to find what was happening socially or intellectually. Neither was church a fun place. The church seemed to be the place where creative ideas go to die. At the center of the church experience was this idea of God, which, by now, was a foreign concept to me. By that I mean that "God" was an idea that I wrestled with, but an idea that I definitely did not own. "God" was somebody else's idea, and I didn't know what to do with it. I remember asking Sunday school teachers, "If God created the heavens and the earth, who created God?" None of them seemed to have an answer. This and similar frustrating questions led me to the conclusion that they were giving me doctrine uncoupled from reality. They seemed to have learned how to tell the Bible stories, but they didn't know the key figure, God. Was God really just a learned concept, or was He real?

When my father and I got into a lengthy and heated debate as to whether or not God existed, lasting well into the night, I kept throwing out questions and scenarios, to which my father seemed stumped for answers. My father gave up in frustration. Feeling I had won the argument, proving that God didn't really exist, I began calling myself an atheist. In truth, I felt there had to be some good reason for thousands of years of God talk, but I just couldn't see God. I wanted someone to make me able to see God.

In the August 2018 issue of *Christianity Today*, a Pew Research poll digs into why people go to church. "The most important reason for going: to become closer to God. Yet 1 in 5 adults who attend monthly or more say they do not usually feel God's presence; 1 in

4 don't usually feel a sense of community; and 4 in 10 don't usually feel connected to their faith's history" (Weber 2018).

So, the poll found that for 81% of regular church goers, a major reason for church attendance is to become closer to God, yet 20% don't feel God's presence; they don't really meet God in church. These are Christians who regularly attend church, defined in the poll as those who attend monthly or more. Like many answers to polls, many of those who claim to feel God's presence are telling the pollster the answer they think they should be giving. Therefore, it is likely that the numbers of those who do not really feel the presence of God is even higher. How does someone attend church year after year but never experience the presence of God?

This failure to see God manifested in Christian or Jewish practice is the reason that theologians have formulated the "Death of God" theology. To be clear, Harvey Cox does not suggest God is dead in his book *The Secular City*, he only says that religion is becoming irrelevant. Thomas J.J. Altizer is the most radical proponent of the "Death of God" theology. Altizer believed that the transcendent God had incarnated as Jesus Christ, and remains as an "immanent spirit" through the Church following Christ's death (Altizer 1966).

The problem, whether or not God is with us or relevant, is compounded for Jewish believers who rely on our Old Testament, in which God is very much in control of history. Richard Rubenstein became another frequent visitor to Unification Theological Seminary, where I first encountered him. Rubenstein, who became more closely linked to the Unification Church as time went on, wrote *After Auschwitz*, which was published the year after Cox's *Secular City*. In it, Rubenstein concludes that it is no longer possible to see God as being in control of history. He says, "I believe the real question should be *not how we speak of God without religion*, but *how we speak of religion in the time of the death of God*" (Rubenstein 1966, 205).

The Holocaust, Rubenstein concludes, wars against any thought of a benevolent God guiding history for His good purposes. He is hardly the only Jewish theologian to reject the biblical view of God. "Any attempt at theodicy [vindicating God's goodness in history] in the face of the full horror of the [Holocaust] is impermissible, even more, it is blasphemy" (Katz 1983, 143). Another Jewish theologian suggests, "the Holocaust may be a radical rupture in history—and that among things ruptured may not just be this or that way of philosophical or theological thinking, but thought itself" (Fackenheim 1982, 193).

Neither Cox nor Rubenstein are atheists. In fact, very few, if any, of the death of God theologians would say that God does not exist. A better way of phrasing things, though less provocative, would be to say: God is irrelevant to society as a whole. "'God is dead' refers less to God than to humanity" (Rubenstein 1966, 246). I believe that the problem of the social relevance of God pre-existed the Holocaust, but the horror of the Holocaust took our breath away, deepening the doubt about the good and shepherding God.

How do we answer the question of the Holocaust? How do we face the many manifestations of radical evil at work in this world today? Modern man has taken full control of his destiny, for better or, far too often, for very much worse. God seems to have become an irrelevant factor. The secular city has pushed God out of the picture. In all of this the awful question persists, where is God? Why doesn't God save us from ourselves?

Reframing God

My own questions and doubts about God came to seem trivial compared to those of others who have suffered incredible injustice. I did some work for a Jewish man who was sent as a teenager with all the money his family could muster to the United States. His objective was to raise enough money to bring another family member, and then another, and so on. By the time he had raised the money for the first, his entire family had been rounded up and sent to concentration camps. He had no way to contact them or to save them. He never saw or heard from any of them again. They all became victims of the Holocaust.

It is not comfortable to try to grapple with the world as it is and to try to find God in it. And so Nietzsche's Zarathustra, sitting atop his lonely mountain, couldn't avoid the question, where is God? For those growing up outside of the church or religion the question is less pressing. But I grew up in church, so the question was unavoidable.

My first baby step came at my first weekend with the Moonies. I cornered one of the instructors and asked my favorite question, "If God created the heavens and the earth, who created God?" He replied, "No one. He is the first cause of all things." He had reframed my vision of God using a classic proof of God. Suddenly, it was easy to see the hand of God in all things. As Paul puts it, "For the invisible things of him from the creation of the world are clearly seen, being understood by the things that are made, even his eternal power and Godhead" (Romans 1:20).

I love the outdoors and happened to be living in a great place for appreciating creation. What this man had suggested made perfect sense to me. At this time I was living in Missoula, Montana, nestled in the Rocky Mountains, surrounded by ski slopes and clear running rivers. This was the location for the movie "The River Runs Through It." I would fly fish for my supper, and ran the rapids in a canoe all throughout my college days. It was easy to see the loving hand of God in the creation around me.

Framing the issue this way, it was difficult for me to imagine that all of that beauty was an accident. What I had to do was to quit looking at the world of our human creation and to see the world that God made. Questions of the Holocaust, the Trail of Tears, the Viet Nam War were questions concerning the actions of humankind. It is worth the time to get out of the city and visit a national park. Look and see the world that God created.

One of the problems is that much of scripture paints a picture of God as a massive humanoid on a throne in the sky, at least that is the picture that I got from my Sunday school lessons. This imagery comes from prophetic visions in the Bible, but it does not sit well with post-Enlightenment thinking. However, we still have to have a way of talking about a God that no one can actually see, touch, taste, smell or feel, and what we do see is God in action in the natural world around us. The heart of God is in every tree and every flower, in butterflys and bunnies. Even pestilence like rats and cockroaches are marvelous little monsters.

God is Alive

My professor of theology at Unification Theological Seminary was Herbert W. Richardson. He had written a response to Harvey Cox's *Secular City* and to "death of God" theology in 1967. In his book *Toward An American Theology,* Richardson suggests that widespread atheism or apathy toward a belief in God is endemic in how we think currently. The basic assumptions that we live by, the attitudes and feelings we share, all the complex tangle of thoughts and emotions we have in common he calls our *intellectus.* Richardson suggests that our intellectus is changing because the world we live in is radically changing. Like the Enlightenment or the Industrial Revolution, we are going through a time of technological revolution, which is causing social revolution. Richardson refers to the new intellectus that is currently being shaped as the "socio-technical intellectus." This new intellectus requires a new way to envision God. He is saying that we have to have a description of God at work in this current world which makes sense to a world which has lost its sense of God.

Secularism is humanity losing faith in the faith of our fathers and trying to find something in itself to lean on. "The modern name for idolatry is 'secularism.' Secularism is an attitude towards reality by which men live (think, act, feel) as if the world existed through itself alone" (Richardson 1967, 35). Secularism is humankind taking responsibility for life because we have no other choice as we see it. My answer to secularism is simple: if Rubinstein's *After Auschwitz* calls into question a benevolent God, how much more does it call into question our human solutions? Is not the Holocaust itself a really horrid human answer to a human problem? Richardson points out that secularism as a philosophy or a theology is a failing answer desperate for a solution.

Richardson's reasons that as our world changes, how we think of the world changes. This in turn requires a shift in how we think of God. It isn't that God is changing; we are. Christians, he reasons, have to get out in front of these changes. "My proposal that Christianity affirm and shape a socio-technical intellectus is not based on any preference for this intellectus, but on recognition of its inevitability" (Richardson 1967, 29). If Christians don't provide a sensible way to envision God in today's world, then the void will be filled with pop culture, self-will and the idol of the month.

How we think about God is important. My experience and Richardson's argument suggest that most people really want to believe in God. Unfortunately, the very people that should be helping them, pastors, church members, theologians and so on, are seemingly unable to communicate with the majority of people in the Western World. That was my experience. It was only my own tenacity to find answers, in spite of the church and not because of the church, that kept me coming back, not to church, but to Christian thought.

Richardson goes on to attempt his own framework for a new theological outlook. At the heart of his message is that "salvation" is only the first step back to God. God's purpose is to bring us into a Sabbath rest: an ability of the body of Christ to join in truly knowing and enjoying the glory of God. Much of his argument relies heavily on the work of Jonathan Edwards, particularly Edwards' book *Concerning the End for Which God Created the World* (Edwards 1765). We'll explore this idea of a Sabbath rest for God's people in later chapters, but, first we have to dig into the question, "Why does humanity require salvation," starting with the Moonie version of salvation. It is necessary to explore Unificationist thought contrasted with Christian thought before getting into some of my experiences as a Moonie confronting Christians.

CHAPTER THREE

THE FALL

All Have Sinned

As a Moonie out on the street, it was common for me to run into Christians. I ran into three young men at a mall who we would label as fundamentalist Christians. They were eager to engage a cultist, sure that they could defeat me in argument. For Moonies, sin and sin nature is huge, so after getting them to assure me that they were born-again Christians, I opened with my standard question, "Do you sin?" The answer was the Bible quote: "All have sinned and fall short of the glory of God" (Romans 3:23). Whether we are talking about Moonies, Christians, Jews or Muslims, sinful human nature is the biggest issue between ourselves and God. Obviously, there are some huge differences between us concerning how to deal with that sin nature. Those differences also set Christians against Christians, and Muslims against Muslims.

Jesus saves! These three young men had that tattooed on their heart. When asked, I suppose they would tell me that Jesus saves us from the flames of hell. If I pressed harder, they would tell me that all who fail to accept Jesus into their heart are doomed to hell. But why? How many of the people on the street of a modern Western nation are concerned about going to hell?

If I am to say that I am saved, I should have to answer the question, "Saved from what?" Why do we assume that all have sinned? Have little babies sinned? Little children? If we are all sinful: why?

In the aggregate, it is easy to see the sinfulness of human behavior. The Holocaust, the Gulag Archipelago, or Mao's Great Leap Forward are all glaring examples of the utter failure of our enlightened human leadership. Ancient history is no better. I was trying to recruit a young man in the Museum of Natural History in NYC. He was under the impression that the lives of primitive men and women were somehow more ideal. This was the philosophy of Rousseau, who in addition did not believe in original sin. We were standing in front of a case of Northwest Coast Indian artifacts. As I grew up in Alaska, I studied their culture somewhat. I pointed to a series of clubs with oblong stones fastened into the end. I asked, "Do you know what those are?" He did not. I said, "Those are slave killers. It was common for the natives of this region to kill as many as forty slaves at a time by punching a hole in the back of their head with these clubs. They would be dumped into a pit to dedicate a new lodge house or other important event."

It is not God's failure, it is ours. Particularly in the case of Germany, we are talking of one of the most advanced of Western countries, committing atrocities on an massive scale. The ingredients present in Germany where present in the United States: a eugenics movement and racism.

How we deal with our sinful flesh has to start with how we sons of Adam got sinful in the first place. If you haven't noticed yet, I am not afraid to wade into controversial territory. These questions sparked some early doctrinal issues within the early Roman church. The Moonies bizarre Christology starts with this issue, which revolves around the story of Adam and Eve in the Garden of Eden as recounted in the Book of Genesis. Before getting into some better understandings of the story, my own included, it would be helpful to look at how Moon and the Unification Church viewed the story of the Garden of Eden and our fall from grace.

An Apple on a Tree

We get the story which we refer to as the Fall of Man from the Book of Genesis, chapter three. Adam and Eve partake of fruit forbidden to them, the fruit from the Tree of the Knowledge of Good and Evil. At this moment, the two, our first human ancestors, fall from the grace of God. What is this fall from grace?

Like many of the topics in this book, the importance of the Fall may not seem to be immediately obvious. Christians quite often proclaim that, "Jesus saves," but can't always answer the follow up question, "saves from what?" Biblically, theologically, the answer is the Fall of humankind from the grace of God and the subsequent expulsion from Eden. Even an anti-theistic belief system like Communism follows the basic formula: Eden, to the fall from grace, and back to heaven on earth.

I have to admit that even as a Moonie, for whom the Fall of humankind is central to their theology, I really had no appreciation for the importance of this story. Having rinsed my brain from Sun Myung Moon's version, and getting a clear handle on the Biblical version, I can definitely now see how significant this chapter of Genesis really is. Let me start with the story as Moses tells it. The story starts with the snake in the Tree of the Knowledge of Good and Evil talking Eve into sampling the fruit on the tree.

> Now the serpent was more crafty than any other beast of the field that the LORD God had made. He said to the woman, "Did God actually say, 'You shall not eat of any tree in the garden'?" And the woman said to the serpent, "We may eat of the fruit of the trees in the garden, but God said, 'You

shall not eat of the fruit of the tree that is in the midst of the garden, neither shall you touch it, lest you die.'" But the serpent said to the woman, "You will not surely die. For God knows that when you eat of it your eyes will be opened, and you will be like God, knowing good and evil." So when the woman saw that the tree was good for food, and that it was a delight to the eyes, and that the tree was to be desired to make one wise, she took of its fruit and ate, and she also gave some to her husband who was with her, and he ate. (Genesis 3:1-6).

The story goes on, Adam and Eve are soon ejected from Eden and blocked from access to the Tree of Life. But, before we tackle that, let us look at the immediate results, starting with the Unificationist version of events.

They Knew They Were Naked

Immediately after the Fall, the story continues, "Then the eyes of both were opened, and they knew that they were naked. And they sewed fig leaves together and made themselves loincloths" (Genesis 3:7). God then comes into the garden. He looks for the couple, who have hidden themselves:

But the LORD God called to the man and said to him, "Where are you?" And he said, "I heard the sound of you in the garden, and I was afraid, because I was naked, and I hid myself." He said, "Who told you that you were naked? Have you eaten of the tree of which I commanded you not to eat" (Genesis 3:9-11)?

According to Sun Myung Moon, this indicates that the forbidden fruit on the tree is sex. The *Divine Principle* (DP 1973, DP referring to *Divine Principle,* which does not list an author) is the Moonie guide to the Bible. In the *Divine Principle*, the Fall of Man began when Lucifer seduced Eve sexually in the garden. Eve went on to seduce Adam into having premarital sex.

The Unificationist has a unique interpretation of the two trees found in the Garden of Eden: the first tree, the Tree of Life, represents Adam according to their teaching (DP 1973, 67-68). Because of the Fall, Jesus was meant to come as the replacement for Adam so that Jesus would become the Tree of Life (DP 1973, 69). In the Unification Church's theology, Jesus was meant to restore the original sinless bloodline. Jesus failed to restore Adam's bloodline since he was crucified before he was able to get married and raise a family. Unification theology says that the second coming (Moon) is meant to replace Jesus and establish the Kingdom of Heaven on Earth, thus becoming the Tree of Life (DP 1973, 69) and establishing the sinless bloodline.

In Unificationism, what is the Tree of the Knowledge of Good and Evil? It is Eve (DP 1973, 69). The fruit on Eve's tree is her sexuality (DP 1973, 74). All this begs the question, why call the trees "of life" and "of the knowledge of good and evil?" Shouldn't they be called the Tree of Man and the Tree of Woman? Unificationism is skewed to suggest that sexual dysfunction is the root of all evil. There are respected Christian commentators who believe the sin in the garden was sexual, so the doctrine is not heretical necessarily. However, most commentaries suggest the sin is rebellion, disobedience to God, or a seduction to ignore the command of God. To be clear, there is no specific doctrine covering the details of the Fall that is common to all Christians.

F.B. Meyer, in his commentary on the Fall suggests:

> The order of temptation is always the same. The
> Tempter without, and within the strong desire

for sensual gratification, with the secret hope
that somehow the consequences may be avoided.
The eye inflames passion; passion masters the
resistance of the will; the body obeys its impulse;
the act of gratification is followed immediately
by remorse and guilt. Then we need the second
Adam (Meyer 1914)!

He refers to sensual gratification, but not specifically sexual
gratification. A suggestion of sexual gratification appears to
stretch the meaning of the passage. The Moonies will counter
that Adam and Eve covered themselves in leaves to hide their
nakedness (Genesis 3:7), indicating a sexual transgression.

I had a friend and teacher who had been a pediatrician for
many years. He always said the first child can come at any time,
after that they all take nine months. His wry humor admitted
that people aren't always good at saving themselves for marriage.
I don't advocate premarital sex, but there are worse sins: Cain
killing Abel, for instance (Genesis 4:8). How does the murder of
Abel follow from Adam and Eve's sexual missteps? I don't think
it does. We will return to that thought.

In the introduction to the *Divine Principle,* adultery is
claimed to be "the greatest of all sins" according to Christian
doctrine (DP 1973, 7). As we have seen, this is easily true from
the Moonie perspective, but from the Christian perspective?
I am not sure what doctrine is being referred to because I am
not aware of any doctrine that ranks sins from better to worse.
Paul, rather, suggests that the sins of this world, the sins of the
flesh, stem from a failure to glorify God and loss of faith in the
goodness of God's designs. The opening chapter of the Book of
Romans describes a descent into darkness which starts from
a failure to lean into God. Our fall from grace starts with our
interrupted relationship with God, not from any particular sin
of the flesh:

And since they did not see fit to acknowledge God, God gave them up to a debased mind to do what ought not to be done. They were filled with all manner of unrighteousness, evil, covetousness, malice. They are full of envy, murder, strife, deceit, maliciousness. They are gossips, slanderers, haters of God, insolent, haughty, boastful, inventors of evil, disobedient to parents, foolish, faithless, heartless, ruthless. Though they know God's righteous decree that those who practice such things deserve to die, they not only do them but give approval to those who practice them (Romans 1:28-32).

The strongest thing that the Moonies had going for them was a desire to bring people together centered on God. That coupled with a willingness to sacrifice meant that the Moonies were predisposed to shun the self-centered ways of the Fall, as listed above. The Moonies did have a strong sense of their absolute rightness, which I wouldn't condemn outright. The closer a person comes to a deep personal relationship with God, the more likely a person is to have a conviction of being in the right place. When Peter speaks with conviction before the Sanhedrin (Acts 4:8-12), the learned men governing religious affairs were stunned by the confidence of the disciples: "Now when they saw the boldness of Peter and John, and perceived that they were uneducated, common men, they were astonished. And they recognized that they had been with Jesus" (Acts 4:13). Why? The Jewish leaders were already familiar with Jesus' ability to defeat their top debaters through intelligent questions and answers: "And after that no one dared to ask him any more questions" (Mark 12:34).

Self-confidence is expected from those close to God. That doesn't mean that self-confidence is warranted in every case. Hopefully, I would like to show, that a Moonie's confidence in

Moon's theology is definitely not warranted. The Fall involves something entirely different, a self-centered way of thinking. Often self-centered thought is anything but self-confident. Self-centered thought separates my people group or myself from all others.

The Tree of Life

I began my religious quest in earnest, starting in 1970 when I entered college. I discovered several books that used the Tree of Life image from the Genesis account to discuss how humankind places itself at the center of all religious imagery. Peter Berger's *The Sacred Canopy* (Berger 1967), as well as works by Mircea Elliade, Carl Jung, Bruno Bettelheim, and Joseph Campbell, come immediately to mind. These were authors that were taking religious imagery and breathing new life into them.

Religious imagery was appearing in movies, in music and in popular psychology and sociology, almost always removed from the original Biblical context. It was great fodder for thought and lent an aura of timeless importance. But, as I look back on all that quasi-religious talk, I also think it was greatly depleting the significance of the imagery. So, let's look at the Tree of Life in the context of Genesis.

The two trees in the garden, the Tree of Life and the Tree of the Knowledge of Good and Evil, are a contrast. One is desirable, the other is not. We know that the Tree of the Knowledge of Good and Evil is forbidden by God (Genesis 2:17). That should make it undesirable for Adam and Eve and all their descendants. The Tree of Life was desirable, but after the Fall access was cut off for all of humanity (Genesis 3:24). The two trees stand in the middle of the garden. Out of the garden flow four rivers which supply the abundance of the Middle East and North Africa. Two of these we know, the Tigris and the Euphrates, which flow from modern Turkey through modern Iraq, long known as the cradle of civilization. The other two are hotly debated. One of the remaining two flows through a land with ample gold and precious stones. What is clear is that these are rivers that supply abundance.

Biblically, the Tree of Life is associated with wisdom, with healing, and with abundance:

> Blessed is the one who finds wisdom, and the one who gets understanding, for the gain from her is better than gain from silver and her profit better than gold... She is a tree of life to those who lay hold of her; those who hold her fast are called blessed (Proverbs 3:13-14,18).

> The fruit of the righteous is a tree of life, and whoever captures souls is wise (Proverbs 11:30).

> a desire fulfilled is a tree of life (Proverbs 13:12).

> through the middle of the street of the city; also, on either side of the river, the tree of life with its twelve kinds of fruit, yielding its fruit each month. The leaves of the tree were for the healing of the nations (Revelations 22:2).

Clearly the Tree of Life is not merely symbolic of life, but of abundant life. So how do we lock into this abundant life? The Book of Revelation helps here: "He who has an ear, let him hear what the Spirit says to the churches. To the one who conquers I will grant to eat of the tree of life, which is in the paradise of God" (Revelations 2:7). And again: "Blessed are those who wash their robes, so that they may have the right to the tree of life and that they may enter the city by the gates" (Revelations 22:14). Directly following the latter is this warning: "if anyone takes away from the words of the book of this prophecy, God will take away his share in the tree of life and in the holy city, which are described in this book" (Revelations 22:19).

As a side note poking holes in the Unificationist idea that the Tree of Life represents Adam, note that Proverbs 3:18 says, "She is a tree of life." Wisdom is represented as female in scripture.

By laying out the Moonie perspective and the biblical perspective, I am hoping that it is clear that the starting point of one's theology can seriously taint how one approaches God and religion. For the Moonie, all human ills start with sex, and therefore a tainted bloodline. Restore the bloodline, and those of the new bloodline are now perfectly restored to God's original intention. As we will see, this does not seem to have been the case with Sun Myung Moon's family, therefore it is unlikely that any of his followers have reaped the desired benefits either.

The Knowledge of Good and Evil

Now let's take a closer look at the Genesis account concerning the Tree of the Knowledge of Good and Evil:

> And the LORD God commanded the man, saying, "You may surely eat of every tree of the garden, but of the tree of the knowledge of good and evil you shall not eat, for in the day that you eat of it you shall surely die" (Genesis 2:16-17).

> But the serpent said to the woman, "You will not surely die. For God knows that when you eat of it your eyes will be opened, and you will be like God, knowing good and evil" (Genesis 3:4-5).

What is at the center of this account? It is the desire of Adam and Eve to know for themselves what is good and what is evil.

Following their sampling of the fruit, Adam and Eve could go on living perfectly "good" in all their activities, but completely out of God's will by metering their lives on the standard laid out by *their own understanding of good and evil*, that is, by their own knowledge of what it means to be good or evil. The issue has never been about good versus evil. It has always been an issue of God's will versus my will. We have been living by the seat of our own pants, since Adam and Eve and it still isn't working. That is the crux of the argument.

Dietrich Bonhoeffer's *Ethics* begins with this very problem of trying to define good and evil. For Bonhoeffer, any ethics based on trying to define good vs. evil is not Christian. His opening statement, the very first sentence, declares:

> The knowledge of good and evil seems to be the aim of all ethical reflection. The first task of Christian ethics is to invalidate this knowledge (Bonhoeffer 1955, 21).

In a footnote to these opening lines, Bonhoeffer makes clear that using other terms to change how a person weighs what is right and what is wrong, as several ethicists do, does not change the equation. Christian ethics is not built on the questions and answers defining right and wrong. Christian ethics is built on the body and the blood of Jesus Christ, with its one command: believe.

When Jesus says, "Judge not, that you be not judged" (Matthew 7:1), this is not a warning to prudence in judgment. This is Jesus saying, "Do not judge." For us to judge, we must know God's perfect will. We cannot do that by using our own analysis of what seems to us to be morally correct.

> Knowing good and evil, man is essentially a judge. As a judge he is like God, except that every judgment he delivers falls back on himself. In

attacking man as a judge Jesus is demanding the conversion of his entire being, and He shows that precisely in the extreme realization of his good he is ungodly and a sinner. Jesus demands that the knowledge of good and evil be overcome; He demands unity with God (Bonhoeffer 1955, 34).

Man becomes like God, as the devil suggests (Genesis 3:5), but does not stand in God's position or in God's wisdom. Therefore, the person who judges based on their own understanding is doomed and banished. They stand outside of the garden where God lives. They stand separated from their own salvation. Bonhoeffer's solution is to return to God and to live in His perfect will. Any attempt to rectify the ills of the world through law, even the laws of the Bible, fails. The best Pharisee was still outside of God's will until he turned to join Jesus. At that point, the law is set aside in the union with Jesus:

> the law was our guardian until Christ came, in order that we might be justified by faith. But now that faith has come, we are no longer under a guardian, for in Christ Jesus you are all sons of God, through faith (Galatians 3:24-26).

When Sun Myung Moon suggests that the Tree of Knowledge of Good and Evil is Eve (DP 1973, 69), and that the fruit of the tree is her sexuality (DP 1973, 74), the work of Jesus Christ is undone. We are returned to our familiar world of do and don't. Moonies aren't the only ones who live under the heavy gaze of religious do and don't do. Many, if not most, Christians are locked into a world of do and don't.

So when I, as a Moonie arguing with Christians at the mall or wherever, after eliciting that they do still sin, I followed up by pulling out my Gideon's Bible and reading the entirety of chapter six of Romans, which begins "What shall we say then? Are we to continue in sin that grace may abound? By no means! How can we who died to sin still live in it" (Romans 6:1-2)? This was enough to confound the three young Christians.

Like most Christians, I assume they had become complacent with their sin. By quoting, "all have sinned..." they seemed to be letting themselves off the hook. As Paul is pointing out, having your sins forgiven is not a license to continue to sin. The three young men shifted back and forth on their feet for a bit, and then disappeared. Far too often, Christian preaching and teaching fails to address the need and the process of sanctification. The Moonie solution was to keep trying harder and to spend hours in fasting and prayer, which isn't a bad start. But Moon's understanding of the Fall led to some very strange ideas on the role of Jesus Christ, and how Jesus saves completely. These young men were nowhere near ready to straighten my theology out.

Cain and Abel

In chapter four of the Book of Genesis, we find the first story of a clearly defined sin, the murder of Abel by his brother Cain. The two are the sons of Adam and Eve. They both make offerings to God from the fruit of their labors, Cain from the grain he has planted and harvested and Abel from the herds that he shepherds. God has no regard for Cain's offering, but accepts Abel's offering (Genesis 4:4-5). Cain is understandably upset. What is less understandable is that Cain becomes angry with his brother and not with God. And so, God intervenes at this point to say,

> Why are you angry, and why has your face fallen? If you do well, will you not be accepted? And if you do not do well, sin is crouching at the door. Its desire is for you, but you must rule over it (Genesis 4:6-7).

The story is familiar. Cain chooses to disregard God's warning and to end his disgrace by killing his brother Abel. So, how does this murder follow from sexual misdeeds, as the Unificationists claim? Naturally speaking, it does not. Only by convoluted explanations are the Unificationists able to explain the progression.

But, that murder does follow naturally from having a personal opinion, not God's opinion, as to what is right and wrong. God tries to dissuade Cain, but Cain refuses to listen (Genesis 4:6-7). Do we not tell each other to, "Follow your own heart?" Well, that is what Cain did. He should have listened to God, but instead he followed his own heart.

"Trust in the LORD with all your heart, and do not lean on your own understanding" (Proverbs 3:5). This theme runs steadily through the scriptures. "You keep him in perfect peace whose mind is stayed on you, because he trusts in you" (Isaiah 26:3). Faith is another word for this trust. If my faith is in my race, I become a racist. If my faith is in my nationality, then it is my country against the world. If my faith is in my ethnic heritage, or religious heritage, then all others are lesser in my opinion.

Everyone born of Adam and Eve starts with the disposition to trust their upbringing and what that stirs in them to choose. For me, I grew up a well-educated American with a dry and lackadaisical faith. We dressed up and went to church every week, and the rest of the week was ours. I was trained to be virtuous and keep my integrity. I knew many stories of those who broke with tradition or authority and were heralded for their virtues, whether my Protestant forebears, or the founding fathers of my country, so it was only natural for me to break from expectation and follow my own path. This started with my choice to stop going to church. I adopted a "show me" attitude towards God and the Church.

Where I to transfer my faith from the dictates of my own heart, my personal opinions or prejudices, to a trust in the leadership and guidance of God the Father, Jesus Christ and the Holy Spirit, the curse of self-centered opinion would have been broken. Instead, I was desperately trying to find my own path to virtue.

Original Sin

There are several ways in which the actual nature of the sin in the garden becomes important. The nature of the Fall, also known as the doctrine of Original Sin, governs whether or not the guilt for the sin of Adam and Eve is passed down to the children, and to the children's children, and so on and so on. It also describes the actual effect on all of us who descend from Adam (i.e. everybody). The belief that the guilt of Adam's sin is passed down to us today is largely confined to the Western church, but all Christians believe the effects of our first ancestors sin do affect us.

Because of its implications for the freedom of the will, the issue of original sin came to a head when a monk from Roman occupied England by the name of Pelagius (AD 360-418) attacked Augustine's view that original sin meant that there was no way for a person to be free of sin without the grace rendered on the cross by Jesus. In Augustine's view, all sin and death were the result of the original sin of Adam and Eve (Genesis 2:17 & 3:19; 1 Peter 1:23). He taught that without Christ our minds are darkened and can never attain salvation. Pelagius countered, we are born without sin and are given the free choice to follow or not to follow God's will. Pelagius' view seemed to leave the door open to salvation without the intervention of Christ. Pelagius and his most significant follower, Celestius, were excommunicated in 418. Pelagianism was declared a heresy by the council of Ephesus in 431. Augustine's emphatic belief that original sin leaves a stain on all people until it is removed by baptism in Jesus Christ is a core belief for most Western Christians.

As described above, the doctrine of original sin is built into the foundation of Unification theology, but in a different way; in particular, the belief that the sin started with a sexual relationship between Satan, symbolized by a serpent, and Eve. The Unificationist view is that the human bloodline is tainted from the beginning by that relationship. Ultimately, Moon's understanding of Christ depends on reversing the sexual sin committed in the garden. This twists the Unificationist christology to that of restoring the bloodline of Adam, "the root of sin lay in having received evil blood because of adultery" (DP 1973,75). Our blood, Moon claimed, was tainted by sin. I'll dig into Unificationist christology deeper in a later chapter.

I believe most Christians are like myself in that I grew up with very little understanding of Original Sin or how my life might be tainted by it. I certainly wouldn't want to be judged by Adam's failure, or my father's failures for that matter. That doesn't mean that my father's failures or Adam's failures do not heavily impact my life and therefore my standing in God's eyes, but as a young man I didn't see the significance. As a Moonie, I am not sure that the bloodline arguement was all that convincing either. I simply accepted it and moved on.

For Augustine and many other significant church leaders, a child who dies without having been baptized is excluded from the kingdom of heaven (John 3:3&5). The New Testament is less definitive regarding children. Jesus seems to embrace them whole-heartedly. I believe this is for a very good reason: little children are not able to understand the difference between their own volition and God's desire. They don't know what is good and what is evil. They are not able to lay aside their own understanding, to embrace God's will. They are not able to die to themselves (Galatians 2:20). A little child does not have a language for self-sacrifice.

Clearly everyone is born under the curse of Adam, if for no other reason than they are born into a world of self-interest. A growing child learns the ways of the world. This world teaches them how to stand their ground and to become their own man or woman. By Jesus, the second Adam, anyone can be reborn free of the curse. God's grace allows us to repent of the curse, to choose Jesus as Lord and saviour, and be born anew in Christ (1 Corinthians 15:42-49). But, then comes the long process of learning how to unwind thousands of years of dining on the fruit of the knowledge of good and evil.

My viewpoint now, that Original Sin is the choice to act upon my personal opinion without any input from God, does track well with all of the troubles that we struggle with in this world, whether we are concerned with quarrels in politics, religious warfare, or bullying in the public schools. On a practical level, I cannot say whether or not Adam's failure is baked into my DNA, but I can definitely say it is baked into my culture and all of my social interactions.

For mainline, Bible believing Christians, restoration is accomplished through placing all of our trust in Jesus Christ, who in turn placed all of His trust in God the Father. Based on my own analysis of scripture, I would say that this process is twofold: it involves turning from immoral lifestyles, and then, a surrender of self-directed life, including a religiously inspired self-directed life. "Truly, I say to you, unless you turn and become like children, you will never enter the kingdom of heaven" (Matthew 18:3). The process involves our choice to draw near to God (Hebrews 7:25; James 4:8).

CHAPTER FOUR

POWER TO CHOOSE

Destiny's Child

Regardless of our basic understanding, we will all agree that the Fall involves a poor choice on the part of Adam and Eve. The question then arises, can we choose to separate ourselves from their poor choice and so become free of the effects of the Fall, or is outside intervention necessary. This is the issue that underlies the argument between Augustine and Pelagius. The reformer John Calvin follows Augustine's view that we are predestined to our fate. "For those whom he foreknew he also predestined to be conformed to the image of his Son, in order that he might be the firstborn among many brothers. And those whom he predestined he also called, and those whom he called he also justified, and those whom he justified he also glorified" (Romans 8:29-30). Jonathan Edwards advocated an extreme deterministic view, maintaining that we are all locked into our destiny from the beginning of time. His book *Freedom of the Will* (Edwards 1754) forcefully lays out his argument.

I grew up attending a Presbyterian church Sunday school. The Presbyterians have Calvin's view of predestination baked into their doctrines of belief: the Westminster Confession of Faith. The church I grew up in, The Northern Lights Presbyterian Church, was always concerned with the propriety of the Christian, but was not terribly evangelical. I suppose that the idea that "what will be, will be" has been predestined stole the aggressiveness of their evangelism. It is interesting to note that Calvin was aggressively evangelical, planting new churches all across Europe.

In 1591, Jacob Arminius, a Dutch Protestant theologian, began preaching a series on the Book of Romans. His views on Paul's teachings leaned in the direction of Pelagius' emphasis on free will. He emphasized that Christ died for everyone, not just the elect. Moreover, we have a free will by which we can choose the grace of Christ, refuse the grace of Christ, or even, having chosen Christ, change our minds and so choose to fall from grace. Both the Calvinist view, sometimes referred to as five point Calvinism, and Arminianism, as Arminius's views are known, are widely held in the church today. Methodism, for instance, is Arminian, but the Presbyterians are firmly Calvinist. The Eastern churches were less influenced by Augustine, and so they have never formed a theological consensus one way or the other.

I bring up all this controversy simply as background. Whether our choices have been predetermined or not, we still have to choose. We could look at someone who apparently loses their salvation and say that they were never saved, they merely appeared to be saved; or, we could say that they have lost their salvation. The final situation is the same—they are excluded from the grace of God. We live and die either inside of God's grace, or outside of it. Choice may be predetermined, never-the-less, you and I must choose even if what we will choose has already been predestined. The rest of the argument, and there are eloquent speakers on both sides of the debate, would appear to be a tempest in a teapot. I choose to trust God regardless of the consequences, confident, by experience, that the final end is the best outcome. To me the idea that the choice is programmed in seems to defeat the idea of giving me a choice. However, I can agree that that it is possible.

God's Will

If the problem stopped there, we could drop it and move on. Unfortunately, it doesn't stop there. As we saw with Rubenstien's *After Auschwitz* (Rubenstein 1966), Modern history has brought into an uncomfortable focus the idea that God is no longer in charge.

Process theology was also popular at the time that I was in seminary. In some ways, it is possible to suggest that much of the thinking in Process theology is infused into many of the more radical current theologies. I am not interested, nor competent, to debate the refinements of the theology. I merely want to point out that in Process theology, our choices affect how God chooses:

> The God who permitted Auschwitz will permit anything the creatures choose to do. God is not another agent alongside the creatures, God acts only in them and through them (Cobb & Griffin 1976, 157).

> God could have fixed the world on a necessary course. Power allows that. Being could be all that exists or will exist and allow no alternatives. But our human experience of contingency and the press for freedom and self-determination in our time indicate a different notion of God and a more flexible structure to Being-itself... There is no novelty without risk, and we seem to live in a universe capable of accepting the excitement of risk. We should not exclude God from this experience (Sontag 1978).

Why do all these questions matter? Has God already chosen the course of history, as some Bible passages suggest? Or, do we have to make our own choices, as other passages indicate? It matters because we are deciding who sits in the driver's seat in our personal lives and in the various seats of cultural and political power. If I am in the driver's seat, or if I choose a Hitler, or a Lenin, or a Hugo Chávez to lead my country, is God at fault? Did God predetermine my bad choice? As in my answer to the controversy between Arminianism and Calvinism, whether I have a free choice, or whether my choices have been predetermined, I am the one who chooses, for better or for worse. It is possible that I have been programmed to choose badly, but assigning blame for the choice doesn't change the facts.

The entire controversy over who is ultimately choosing obscures the deeper issue. Am I sufficiently in tune with the Holy Spirit to know God's opinion and therefore to let God help me to make the proper Godly choice? Several of our current theological assumptions, such as the above Process theology, put us squarely in the driver's seat, where we have to make choices, where we must sit in council and vote on how to approach issues such as homosexuality or abortion. As I see the issue of the Fall, this is the very same way that Adam and Eve approach good and evil.

In contrast, Jesus is showing us an entirely different way to approach these issues. Through Jesus, we can connect with the Holy Spirit and let his voice be our guide. In the end, we still are making choices, but in this instance, we choose to allow God's voice within us guide us to the best choice. This allows us to co-labor with God. I can't think of anyone better to have with me when my boat is in the storm than Jesus Christ. The only catch is that I have to hear the voice of God to choose His will. In general, this seems simple, read the Bible. But when specific issues arise, we will probably need something more direct.

The Prescription

In a discussion with the disciples, Jesus is speaking of his own impending death. Then, before the disciples can protest, he says,

> If anyone would come after me, let him deny
> himself and take up his cross daily and follow
> me. For whoever would save his life will lose it,
> but whoever loses his life for my sake will save it
> (Luke 9:23-24).

Die to yourself. In practical terms, what does it mean to die to yourself? Does this mean becoming a milk-toast nobody who never puts an opinion forward? Or, does dying to self mean that I blindly follow assumptions of Biblical authority, or my church's authority, or some other religious standard?

As a Moonie, I had given up everything to pursue a sacrificial life building the Kingdom of Heaven here on earth. There is a presumption built into that pursuit. I believed that I was on the right path. While at the seminary, I spearheaded the Congress of World Religions. At one point, my faculty advisor (not a member of the Unification Church) suggested that all religions are equal. I immediately replied that I could not believe that and continue to do what I was doing. What I did believe at the time was that the Moonies had the best possible alternative, but I also believed that working with Christians and even other religions would help our efforts faster than standing in opposition to those groups.

The Unificationist believes that all religions are looking in the same direction, but that some are closer to the truth than others. As a Moonie, I often faced a great deal of opposition, even outright hostility, but had to maintain an openness and humility towards my opposition while still presuming to the rightness of my "better" understanding. The problem is that it was Moon and the Unification Church that I was trusting, not the Spirit of the Living God.

Now, as a Christian, and a few decades more mature, I am riding a different horse. I have a more refined understanding and can see areas of cooperation and places where genuine agreement exists between Christ and the works of non-Christians and of dysfunctional Christians. I also see places where there is no room for compromise. Continued study and self-examination improve my range of possibilities. But, above all that, I have come to respect the need for prayer and devotion, because I need God's direction.

So, back to the question of how does one die to oneself? Making choices that are not tainted by the world or by the views of some intervening authority, be it the church or a pastor, or tainted even by my own limited viewpoint, comes down to placing everything before God, which means that I spend time in prayer and meditation, allowing plenty of time for the Holy Spirit to speak and to guide me. As we will see, it is the Moonies that taught me to pray often, long, and fervently, not the church of my youth.

As a Christian, a former pastor of mine and I came into conflict over a personal issue I was wrestling with. He and I did not see eye to eye on the issue. I took the issue to God in prayer. In this case, I felt strongly that God was telling me to follow the pastor's directions. I protested to God that the pastor was wrong. The answer I got couldn't have been clearer if it had been an audible voice, "I know, but do it anyway." I swallowed my pride and did what I was asked. I had taken this issue to God and let Him be my guide; that is what it means to die to oneself, and let Jesus be Lord.

As a Moonie, I was often ordered to do things which I did not particularly want to do. I submitted to the authority I was under. As I look back, it was good for me at the time, even though I was not under the best authority. I was still not at a place where I could hear the voice of God, and so it was not possible to submit to God directly. Moonie life requires a willingness to sacrifice a great deal of personal discretion, especially during the first several years. Much like a soldier, the Moonie has chosen to allow the mission to outweigh the personal preferences of the moment. I can see that my time as a soldier in Moon's army gave me good training for a future spent in the fellowship of God's good grace.

CHAPTER FIVE

JUSTIFICATION BY ATTENDANCE

Sacrifice

M oonies did not expect to be pampered. Our attitude was that of self-sacrifice. One leader fussing about clutter in the church center and wanted the mess cleaned up called out "We don't have servants, we are servants."

It was not possible to become a full fledged member of the Moonies without being willing to sacrifice comfort, lifestyle, most likely friends and sometimes even family relations. Married couples who joined the church together were expected to live separately until they could be married by Moon himself. A full fledged member was known as an A-member. There were also B-members. These were members who stayed in their communities and stayed in their jobs but attended weekly services and rallies. There were not many of these B-members at the time. These were often members who already had families prior to joining and couldn't drop everything to join Moon's army.

Young recruits were being fashioned into an army of sorts. We gave up most of our worldly possessions which made it easy for us to pack up and move at a moments notice. It was not unusual to leave one city and move several states away with little more than a few hours notice. In fact the date of my departure from the church was partly due to a fear of that happening. My wife to be and I had been planning to leave for several weeks, but were trying to find a place to live and were saving money to live on. Moon called all the seminarians to New York for a New Years Day meeting with him. It was not unusual for these meetings to be the announcement of immediate reassignment to some new campaign. The two of us decided to leave the church before the meeting occurred.

We still didn't have a place to stay, but I was designing a Shakespeare play in a small theater in Manhattan and the owner was gracious enough to allow us to stay there until we could find an apartment. We slept on a foldout bed under the audience risers.

Fundraising teams were the ultimate mobile army. They stayed on the move. The women might crowd into a motel room at night, while the men might sleep in the van. Large city or country campaigns were similar. A large number of Moonies would be sent to the one locality with hundreds sleeping on the floor of larger church centers. Accommodations varied greatly. I remember being sent to New York City in wintertime. I was staying in the Hotel New Yorker, which we referred to as the "Ice Palace". The church had just purchased the hotel, it had been vacant for several years. I am not sure that the boilers were totally functional. In any case, the heat only ran in short spurts. The windows were very old and often had gaps of a half and inch or more. The wind howled through the cracks. We did our best to plug the gaps, but the cold was bone chilling. I slept fully clothed and still shivering. When I returned to the New Yorker several years later, the accommodations were much more favorable.

The Pledge

Moon believed himself to be the second coming of Christ. I will talk more fully about his theology in coming chapters, but for this chapter it will be important to know that he did not believe that faith in Jesus accomplished full release from sin nature. Complete transformation, in his view, was accomplished by attending to the Lord of the Second Advent, himself. This is referred to in the *Divine Principles* as Justification by Attendance (DP 1973, 175).

The Unification Church's army of young people, in Moon's theology, served as the foundation of a new society constructing heaven on earth. This was reinforced by pledges recited every morning before the portraits of Mr. and Mrs. Moon, the "True Parents".

Morning prayer started with bowing to the portrait of Mr. and Mrs. Moon. This was usually a full bow, down on the knees and forehead to the floor. The thumbs and index fingers would be placed together to form a triangle, indicating a holy trinity of God, Moon and his wife. The forth figure implied was the individual member, forming a four-position foundation in a diamond shape. Following that was a pledge of loyalty to the "True Parents". Couples who had been married by Moon in a Blessing ceremony, had a more severe pledge that they would use. This might follow the general pledge or might be reserved for private time. After the pledge, prayer would begin.

Bowing and pledging was familiar to the Koreans and the Japanese among us, as it is the same sort of thing practiced by oriental martial arts dojos, ancestor veneration, and prayers to Buddhist saints or Hindu gods. To the Americans and the Europeans among us, this was fairly exotic. For us it made our worship all that much more interesting.

Spiritual Mothers

Integration and the healing of old societal wounds was one of Moon's pet projects. In particular the wedding together of Korea, Japan and the United States was of providential significance in

Moon's vision of history. He brought several Korean elders to the United States to work with him. Younger Koreans were seldom allowed to leave South Korea because of fear that they would be needed to serve in the military in the case of an attack from North Korea.

Moon was free to bring a large number of Japanese young recruits. Those who picked up English quickly were integrated into the US church. Moon devised a plan to place a Japanese sister in every church center as a "spiritual mother". His idea was to bring about a closer harmony between the oriental and western cultures. These spiritual mothers would usually clean, prepare meals and generally acted in a motherly way. Because many of them spoke very poor English they rarely engaged in the outside activities of the church centers.

Moon was not able to provide enough spiritual mothers to supply every center, so when I was assigned to the state of Wisconsin, the Milwaukee center, the only center in Wisconsin, did not have a Japanese sister in residence. Instead, a Japanese woman, the wife of a prominent leader of the fund-raising teams, was assigned to keep tabs on me and my center.

For the most part, the Milwaukee center was functioning well, but the one sister in the center was unhappy with the way things were going. We were running a successful remodeling business and clearing away debt, but she wasn't fitting well into any of the activities. She complained. When the spiritual mother came to town, she began to give me a dressing down in front of my members. I then took her upstairs to the office and gave her a dressing down for disrespecting me in front of my team. How did she think I would be able to operate without the respect of my membership? She never returned. She would call from time to time to take reports over the phone.

The oriental culture is very much top down and driven by a high regard for honor and respect. This is not typical for Americans. We like to know why we are doing what we are doing, and we may even come up with a better way to accomplish the task. The Asians preferred to be quiet and do as told. We Americans would refer to this between ourselves as the *Bushido code*. Since most of us were young, the Americans were often impulsive and at least to an oriental viewpoint, seemed impertinent and disrespectful. To most other Americans, the Moonies seemed unusually respectful.

I Am Your Brain

Moon himself was often frustrated by the Americans constantly wanting to rethink things. He was quoted in the press as saying, "I am your brain." The quote is accurate. I heard him say this and make other similar statements. The press loved to quote this to suggest that this was some sort of hypnotic suggestion, a part of the overall brainwashing supposed to have been foisted upon naive American youth. In context, he was trying to stop us from stalling out, rethinking decisions, but doing little or nothing. I myself was sitting cross-legged on the floor on the front row of a room full of national and international leaders when Moon proclaimed to the group, "If you are not doing anything, do something." He then kicked me clear off the floor. Moon did not mince words. He was very expressive.

Sun Myung Moon was powerfully charismatic and highly intelligent. He had created a new religious movement of international proportions. He had his own publishing company. He had an international business empire. He had recruited scientists and academics to his cause. And yet he was still a Korean. Sometimes he did things that left the Americans and the Europeans scratching their heads. Since the larger part of the American church was made up of young men and women who had at least some college under their belt, the Bushido code was one of the first things which caused a bit of a bad rub.

I became somewhat famous within the church when I delivered a sermon during morning service which pointed out that most of the Moonies had joined the Unification Church to build the kingdom of heaven on earth, not to become blind followers. There was a strangely surreal atmosphere generated as I spoke. The one to two hundred staff members and seminarians visibly divided into three separate categories as I was speaking. One third could be seen to be dark and angry. It was evident from where I stood that they did not like the message. One third became brighter, almost jubilant with joy at the message. The remainder seemed dumbstruck, as if they weren't sure what to think.

The president of the seminary had been called away that morning, so his second in command, a man much less favorable to talk of independent thought, got up to deliver a rebuttal. The controversy raged hot for several weeks. I would walk into the dining hall and the room would go silent. Very few of my detractors would speak to me. I genuinely appreciated the few that did because that allowed me to clarify my position. I was not calling for rebellion. I was calling for leadership skills that include the ability to think for oneself. Some of my supporters were putting me on an unimaginably high pedestal, which I found to be terribly uncomfortable. Two years later I was approached by a young man whom I had never met. He proudly announced that he was the new Bill Wells at the seminary. I wondered how well he was representing my name.

Discipline Within the Church

When there were genuine laps in discipline within the Unification Church, either moral or in command structure, there was no good mechanism for fixing the breakdown. The problem often solved itself by the individuals in question leaving the church. It was rumored that the leader of one center had created his own unique version of the Divine Principles by which he was meant to sleep with all the women in the center. Apparently, most of the members in the center left membership.

Problems between leaders and their members that couldn't be resolved by discussion, were resolved by moving the members or the leaders from one center to another. The mobility of the Unification movement kept those sorts of issues from occurring too often. As mentioned before, I had one member who didn't like how things were working in my center. She asked to be transferred from that center. She was moved, though I had wished that the issue was resolved in another way.

Moral laps, when the member did wish to remain in membership, were often handled by sending the member to a low-profile assignment, where they wouldn't be seen by most members for some time. In the case of sexual sins, this could be three years or more. After I left the church, because I was in a sexual relationship, in fact I married shortly after leaving the church, friends of mine from the Unification Church would come to me and promise me such an assignment if I returned. Oddly enough, I had two dreams where Moon himself came to me dressed in an Inuit (Eskimo) parka asking me to return and that I would be given such an assignment. I assume the parka was meant to remind me of home. I grew up in Alaska, although there were few Inuits in my hometown Juneau. Koreans do look a lot like Inuits, having the round faces and heavy eyelids characteristic of the Inuit. I assured Moon in my two dreams that I had made up my mind and had no intention of changing it, which is also what I told my friends when they came to call.

I am not aware of any full member of the Unification Church who was thrown out for any reason, although it is possible that it could have happened. We did have situations where non-members had to be removed for disrupting meetings.

By in large, the Unification movement ran on a tight social cohesion around the person and theology of Sun Myung Moon. It was a packaged deal. When a person such as myself fell out of lock step with that world, one could try to find a corner of the church to hide in, but generally the solution was to pack one's bags and leave, which is what I did.

For a large part of the Christian world, especially here in the west, falling out of fellowship is as easy as not showing up for church on Sunday. We have a wide variety of churches to choose from, so it isn't hard to find a new place to worship. As a Moonie, it was a drastic decision involving a loss of almost all of my friendships, my place to live, my daily meals, and called into question the entire trajectory of my life. If only out of habit, I still maintained a Moonie style of prayer and worship for several years after leaving, even though I had very little contact with church members. The few who did come to visit were almost always trying to return me to the fold.

CHAPTER SIX

GOD IS LOVE

Good Religion

The reformers liked to refer to good creedal positions as "good religion." It is popular now for preachers and evangelists, as well as lay members of the Church, to refer to "religion" in the negative. To quote the popular teacher Bill Johnson, "Religion is cruel and it's boring." Does this disdain for "religion" by Christian leaders mean that Harvey Cox's vision of a world devoid of significant religion has come to pass?

Cox refers to two strong trends in urban society: anonymity and mobility. I can choose to introduce myself to my neighbors, or I can choose to stay aloof. I come to know a lot of people in the city in which I live, but to know them all well and to engage with them all on an intimate and personal level is impossible, so I pick and choose who I want to associate with closely. For the rest, I remain intentionally aloof. This isn't meanness or displeasure with them. It is the only practical way for most of us to function. I do know people who seem able to handle an enormous number of close interpersonal relationships, but that isn't me. Even a person living in a small rural village where everyone knows everyone can still pick up a cell phone and enter into a much larger world. The cell phone and social media have broken down the walls of isolation for large numbers of people on this planet.

Equally as significant, that same isolated villager can pack their bags and move to the big city. Living in the big city, a person experiences many different social environments. The work environment is usually quite different from the home environment, which may be quite different from the church environment, and so on.

What this means is that we can now choose who we get to know well. We can choose which church to go to or whether or not to go to church at all. Most of us like that freedom and react badly to those who try to press us with should've and could've. We refer to those people as religious, and we don't mean good religion. This is the "religion" that Bill Johnson and others refer to.

On the surface of it Cox and Johnson would seem to agree:

> The age of the secular city, the epoch whose ethos
> is quickly spreading into every corner of the globe,
> is an age of "no religion at all." It no longer looks
> to religious rules and rituals for its morality or its
> meanings (Cox 2013, 4).

The similarities end with the disdain for religious rules. Cox suggests that the secular city presents, "pragmatic men whose interest in religion is at best peripheral" (Cox 2013, 97). Spiritual or metaphysical matters are of no interest to the secular city.

The new breed of Christian wants to finish ripping away the veil between us and the Holy of Holies. That veil is the religious structures that prevent the body of Christ from accessing the living heart of God. These Christians are the ones who want a revitalized spirituality and a metaphysics based on the knowledge of the Holy. Cox explores this in his 1995 book *Fire From Heaven*.

Wine Skins

While Jesus was here on earth, he spent his ministry years training his disciples how to walk with God. While they were all Jews and observed Jewish customs and holidays, they were known to color outside the lines frequently. The Pharisees clashed with Jesus because he and his disciples often disregarded the legal framework that the Pharisees had erected. Jesus promoted a much looser interpretation of Mosaic law by healing on the Sabbath or picking grain on the Sabbath. At other times he argued for a more intense understanding of the law, equating anger and bitterness with murder, or lust with adultery.

What exactly was happening? Jesus was exposing the heart and meaning of the Law. The laws handed down to Moses were meant to help us to know when we are in step with God and when we are not. They were not meant to empower a new class of social micromanagers. My favorite example is from Deuteronomy 14:1, "You shall not boil a young goat in its mother's milk." Here is a law meant to protect respect for the livestock that feeds us. It has been turned into Kosher law which says dairy based food and meat based foods must be kept strictly separate: different pots and pans, even different serving dishes. The original purpose of the law is lost in the meticulous effort to make sure the law is never violated.

The way that we think, the way that we act in relationship with others and with society as a whole, the way that we treat the world around us and especially how we relate to God are the actual substance of the religious life. The rules, the culture, the creedal statements, or in the case above, the laws of God, are all meant to keep us in proper alignment with God and with each other.

When the disciples of John the Baptist ask Jesus why his disciples don't fast the way they do (Mark 2:18), Jesus answers obliquely: "no one puts new wine into old wineskins. If he does, the wine will burst the skins and the wine is destroyed, and so are the skins. But new wine is for fresh wineskins" (Mark 2:22).

Wine requires a container to keep it. New wine is still very active. Yeasts cause grape juice to ferment, and new wine still has fermentation going on. Therefore, if it is put into old, stiff wineskins and then sealed, the expansion caused by the gas released in the continuing fermentation process will cause the skin to burst.

John the Baptist and his disciples were still living under the shadow of Mosaic Law. But, the Law was about to be transcended; something was "fermenting." Jesus was the answer to the law's purpose. In essence, Jesus was the Law made flesh. Jesus embodied everything that the Mosaic Law was meant to accomplish. Making statements about transforming the legal paradigm is easy, but actualizing what the Law means is to live free of the Law. Actualizing the Law in Jesus can be a long and difficult process. As a Moonie, I was still very attached to religious law.

New Wine Skin

When Harvey Cox wrote *The Secular City*, he had just returned from Germany, where he had spent a year in Berlin. Berlin was still divided between Communist East Germany and Democratic West Germany. He had been involved in religious education on both sides of the Berlin Wall, which had been erected only a few years before. His future vision for religion was influenced by the shadow of Dietrich Bonhoeffer and by the on-going Christian-Marxist dialogue.

Bonhoeffer's *Letters and Papers from Prison* has several letters sketching out thoughts in which he speaks of an end of religion (Bonhoeffer 1967). That, coupled with the Christian-Marxist dialog active during Cox's time in Berlin, gives rise to what I believe is Cox's distorted view of Bonhoeffer:

> In Jesus, God refuses to fulfill either tribal expectations or philosophical quandaries. As

Bonhoeffer says, in Jesus God is teaching man to
get along without Him, to become mature, freed
from infantile dependencies, fully human (Cox
2013, 306).

We have already seen from Bonhoeffer's discussion of ethics
that he is clearly not suggesting that we should take the wheel.
Rather, he suggests that living by our own understanding is the
very root of humanity's problem. So there should be no question
that Bonhoeffer believes that we need God behind the wheel. How
does Cox get it so wrong?

For Cox, in 1965, reconstructing the secular world is the new
face of Christianity. Besides his interest in the Christian-Marxist
dialogue, Cox had been active in civil rights marches and other
activist causes. It is not surprising that his vision for Christianity
going forward is social activism. For Cox, "Jesus Christ comes
to his people not primarily through ecclesiastical traditions, but
through social change" (Cox 2013, 175). I certainly wouldn't want
to suggest that Christians shouldn't be involved in social activism.
Rather, Christians must learn always to take their activism to God
first and be willing that God's answer may be: stand down. Every
good gift comes down from above (James 1:17).

In some ways, the failure of our well-intended reforms to
perform as expected has ushered in a new desire for spiritual
reform. The best place to start with reform is at the place things
started to deviate badly from our desired goals. For many, myself
included, this meant going back to my religious roots because
secularism has failed horribly. I don't think that I am the only one
seeing things that way.

By 1990, when Cox wrote a new introduction to *The Secular
City*, he had to admit that we were in the midst of "an unanticipated
resurgence of traditional religion" (Cox 2013, xli). In 1995, he
published *Fire From Heaven,* a dive into the exploding world of
Pentecostal spirituality. While most of mainline Christianity was

shrinking, something remarkable was happening; the oddball Christians from across the tracks were becoming the new face of Christianity world-wide.

Herbert Richardson also saw that Christianity was at a moment of change. The way the post-industrial child envisioned the world was undergoing radical change. For Richardson, the enormous social changes afoot in the nineteen-sixties were causing the old religious underpinnings to fail under the stress. Cox's secularism, existentialism, the culture wars and so on, were merely a symptom of this changing world in Richardson's view. While the secularists were busy demythologizing Christianity, removing all references that defy scientific reasoning, Richardson points to Kenneth Boulding (*The Image* 1956) and Marshall McLuhan (*Understanding Media* 1964) to suggest that the stories that make up our religious viewpoint cannot be disassembled and reassembled to our liking. How we see God isn't in the logic of the Bible, it is in the poetry of the storied images. The religious logic for the new social situation has to come out of the old stories, not from a reconstructed amalgamation.

More problematic is the desire to take the reins, so to speak, to push God to the side and remake Christianity the way we want it to be. Two books that were very popular at the time were *Man Makes Himself* (Childe 1951) and *The Social Construction of Reality* (Berger and Luckmann 1966). Both books fed the narrative that we, all together, create our world in the sense that how we view the world shapes our every interaction with it. The impression is that religion is a fictitious construction that helps to shape our corporate understanding.

I hadn't read any of these books when I started college in 1970, but due to the strong prevalence of Freudian, Jungian and existential thought, it was definitely the whimsy in the air. I had a lot of questions and I needed answers. So, I began to read. I read psychology, sociology, social anthropology, and religion. I paid particular attention to reading all the books of the great religions: *The Quran, The Vedas, The Diamond Sutra,* and *The Bible.* Very little of this reading was a part of my school work. It was a personal quest. In the end, I had a lot more knowledge, much of it false, but very few answers. The only thing I was certain of is that at the bottom of all the God talk, there is something there. It is not just a made-up control mechanism, as Freud claimed (*Totem and Taboo* 1919).

Christianity Re-imagined

I suppose this is a long and heady introduction, all to say that, for me at the time, the Unification Church seemed to be on the right track. Traditional Christianity had lost its flavor for me. The Unificationist explanations of the Biblical stories were re-imagined in such a way that it sounded logical to an educated mind. The Moonie theology had all the good stuff: patriotism, family values, social action and a willingness to sacrifice for a better world. Not surprisingly, the bulk of Moonie recruiting came from college campuses.

Since the core of Unification Theology was building the Kingdom of God on Earth as in Heaven, it seemed that Jesus had failed to accomplish his goal. For the Moonies, the Cross was to pay the price for a second chance at building the Kingdom of Heaven here on earth. The currency of redemption, according to Moon, was self-sacrifice (indemnity). It was a theology suspended somewhere between Cox's social activism and Richardson's call for Sabbath.

The Moonies reveled in all the negative attention. Persecution of the church was, to the Moonies, a proof positive of their righteous cause. After all, Jesus was persecuted, even to the death on the cross. The Moonies were certain that they were fulfilling the role of Christ's second coming through Sun Myung Moon. Opposition to the establishment of God's Kingdom was to be expected. So, this brings us to the most astounding claim of Moon and the church: Sun Myung Moon is the second coming of Christ.

CHAPTER SEVEN

SECOND COMING

The Bold Claim

Proclaiming oneself to be the second coming of Christ is a rather bold claim. To those with a fundamentalist background or other theologically conservative background, this sounds just plain crazy. Unification theology is liberal theology pushed to the limit. For those who haven't been to seminary, which is most people, let me explain. Liberal theology is not political liberalism, but it does share some of the same DNA.

A recent book on liberal theology offers this definition penned in 1949 by liberal theologian Daniel Day Williams:

> By "liberal theology" I mean the movement in modern Protestantism which during the nineteenth century tried to bring Christian thought into organic unity with the evolutionary world view, the movements from social reconstruction, and the expectations of "a better world" which dominated the general mind. It is that form of Christian faith in which a prophetic-progressive philosophy of history culminates in the expectation of the coming of the Kingdom of God on earth (Dorrien 2001, xiv).

Since I am not intending this to be a deep theological discussion, let me simplify this a bit; liberal theology subordinates scripture and Christian traditions to *scientific* reasoning. Now there may be room for debate on whether some form of evolution is scriptural, but the liberal argument turns the issue on its head, saying, is the Genesis account scientific? The assumption is that if the biblical account is not reasonable to a scientist or philosopher, then we should regard the Genesis account as interesting, but quaint. In other words, we ignore it. We could, as was popular during my time in seminary, *demythologize* the text by removing anything the scientists and philosophers don't like, and then *remythologize* the text by giving it new meaning. This revision of the Biblical worldview is widely practiced today. These forms of liberal, re-imagined gospel accounts range from the willful dismantling of the Bible to suit current tastes, as is seen in Open Theology, to the mild bending to public pressure experienced in many large denominations concerning LGBTQ issues.

Remember, my understanding is that Unification theology has changed significantly since 1982 when I left, so everything I have to say about it has to be put into that context. At that time, the Unification Church was socially conservative, particularly in matters of sex and family. Their doctrine of Christ on the other hand was closer to Unitarian thought, and their understanding of works righteousness seemed to exceed that of the Arminians.

Christology

The Unification doctrine of Christ during my time in the church was that Jesus was a sinless man and therefore perfect according to God's intention in creating humankind (DP 1973, 209). The Unificationist belief was that the Word made flesh meant that the perfect intention of God was realized in the person of Jesus, "Nevertheless, he can by no means be God Himself" (DP 1973,

210-211). In addition, the church did not believe in immaculate conception. I heard Moon himself intimate that he believed Jesus' father was Zechariah, a view put forward by certain Enlightenment philosophers looking for a natural explanation of the virgin birth (Boslooper 1962, 87). This would make Jesus and John the Baptist half-brothers, not just cousins. This would also make Jesus illegitimate. The Unificationist leaves aside the fact that scripture affirms both the divinity of Jesus Christ as well as the virgin birth of Jesus, as do several early church councils, which are considered definitive by Catholic, Orthodox, Coptic, Syrian and Protestant believers.

The Unification view makes Jesus in every way human, and definitely not divine, although he was unique in that he was without sin. Even though the Unificationist will say that Jesus is God incarnate, this for them is basically a poetic gloss. What the Moonie means by this is that when you see Jesus, you see the perfect intention of God. This leaves the door wide open for other "christs." The main Moonie requirement is that the individual is a sinless and perfect representation of God's intention.

In a paper entitled "Unification and Traditional Christology: An Unresolved Relationship," theologian Durwood Foster notes that Unification Christology bears a similarity to that of Paul Tillich (Richardson 1981, 185-187). It isn't strictly orthodox, but it tries to stay close enough. Foster suggests that further refinement by the Moonies themselves may clarify Unificationist distance from or proximity to traditional Christology. The Moonies didn't categorically deny the Nicene Creed with its specific language: "the only-begotten Son of God, begotten of the Father before all worlds (æons), Light of Light, very God of very God, begotten, not made, being of one substance with the Father," but rather skated past it as if it didn't mean what it meant.

Paul Tillich's book *The Courage To Be* (Tillich 1952) was one of my favorites when I was in seminary. I was still fighting with the Existential philosophy I had been sired on, and Tillich described the fight I was in very well, which made that turmoil make sense. However, since I have become a Christian, his description of God as "the ground of Being" seems to really miss the significance of who and what God is to me now. His steeling himself to the existential crises of man is not even close to my current experience. My walk with God, with Jesus, and with the Holy Spirit is a delight, not a fight. At the root of this new experience is that I realize Jesus is more than a really good guy, Jesus is a doorway to a relationship with God the Father, by putting me in touch with the Holy Spirit. That is not head knowledge, but a daily experience.

The second component of the Unification Christology, after answering who is the Christ, is how does Christ save (soteriology). According to Unification Church doctrine, Jesus came to establish the Kingdom of God on earth as it is in heaven (Matthew 6:10). According to the church's teaching, Jesus was supposed to establish an earthly theocracy that would continue forever after his death. In addition, Jesus was meant to marry and have children, establishing an earthly lineage. Salvation was meant to be spiritual and physical.

> Because the Jewish people disbelieved Jesus and delivered him up for crucifixion, his body was invaded by Satan, and he was killed. Therefore, even when Christians believe in and become one body with Jesus, whose body was invaded by Satan, their bodies still remain subject to Satan's invasion (DP 1973, 148).

Jesus failed, so Moon's reasoning went, not because of any imperfection on his part, but because the leaders, specifically the Jewish leaders, failed to rally behind him. This would leave all of humankind under the curse. But, stretching scripture again, Moon's *Divine Principles* say that by sacrificing himself, Jesus was therefore able to pay the price (indemnify, see below) so that spiritual salvation was available to humankind (DP 1973, 151), even if physical salvation was not. Essentially, the atonement on the cross was for the failures of the leadership, particularly the Jewish leadership, and nothing else, in the Unificationist view. As a Moonie, I had a very deep respect for the sacrifice of Jesus, but a totally distorted view of its significance. More importantly, I was not receiving the benefit of knowing Jesus.

The New Testament is clear that complete salvation was accomplished on the cross, which means that our sins are paid for (atoned for). Scripture is quite clear that the Atonement was Jesus sacrificing himself on the cross so that all who come to him could receive complete forgiveness of sins and receive the Holy Spirit of God so that the believer could come to live sin free. This doesn't mean that Satan is unable to attack us. What it does mean is that we can appropriate our salvation, and by our complete trust in Jesus we can overcome Satan's attack. But, in Moon's conception, and therefore the view of Unification theology, the only thing accomplished at the cross was the possibility of a partial salvation. By this line of reasoning, a second coming is necessary not to culminate the age, but to complete the original task. Moon was very clear that he considered that to be his God given mission. He believed himself to be the sinless second Christ tasked with creating the Kingdom of God on earth.

Resurrection

In Christian terms, the Resurrection refers to Christ Jesus's resurrection from the dead after having completed a life of sinless self-sacrifice. The Resurrection is the crowning glory by which Jesus received all authority. For the Moonies, resurrection is something altogether different. They do not believe Jesus was physically resurrected, nor that any of us will be physically resurrected:

> Therefore, "resurrection" means the phenomenon occurring in the process of man's restoration, according to the providence of restoration, from the state of having fallen under Satan's dominion, back to the direct dominion of God. Accordingly, when we repent of our sins, making ourselves better and better, day by day, we are coming closer to resurrection (DP 1973, 170).

In the Unification view, Jesus achieved a spiritual resurrection, but not a physical resurrection. Those who believe in the words of Jesus, "justification by faith," achieve a "life-spirit" stage of resurrection (DP 1973, 175). The perfection stage of restoration is achieved when people believe in and attend to the "Lord of the Second Advent" (i.e. Moon), also referred to as "justification by attendance."

> The spirit men belonging to this age can attain the divine-spirit stage of perfect resurrection in both spirit and body by believing in and serving the Lord of the Second Advent (DP 1973, 175).

Traditional Christian belief says that the cross provides for our atonement from sin, and the resurrection provides for a new life in Christ. A life in Christ is life that has access to the Holy Spirit and therefore an ability to hear God and to know His desires for us. As we walk with the voice of God's Spirit in our ear, our life is changed "from glory to glory" (2 Corinthians 3:18). This is sanctification.

Sanctification

There is no single Christian understanding of sanctification. No sensible Christian believes that we become perfect people the moment we say yes to Jesus. There is a process, which the New Testament writers allude to many times (I Thessalonians 5:23; I Peter 2:5). By this process the Christian becomes more and more sanctified, closer to God the Father and Christ Jesus. For many Christians, this has come to mean adhering to specific rules laid down in church doctrine. I do not believe this is Biblical, as you should be seeing by now. In my understanding of scripture, sanctification means drawing closer to Jesus and allowing the Holy Spirit to work (Philippians 1:6). It is a process, sometimes rapid, sometimes painfully slow, but we are changed, or conformed to the likeness or the image of Christ (Romans 8:29).

Atonement is the price paid to free us from the guilt of our sin toward God. The price is already paid. That is not a process, it is done. Jesus paid the price for you and for me when he hung upon the cross two thousand years ago. The only thing I have to do is step before the throne of grace with my heart turned to Jesus and away from sin and ask for forgiveness. The only thing the thief on the cross next to Jesus did was ask (Luke 23:39-43). He went to his death without a single charge against him in the court of heaven.

Had the thief lived, he would have had to live with a changed heart and attitude. It is not appropriate for those whose sins have been paid for at such a cost to continue to live a sinful lifestyle (Romans 6). This is the issue that I used to confront the young men at the mall.

Changing our lifestyle may involve a radical change to the way a person lives their life. In Moonie terms, this transformation was affected by allegiance and service to Sun Myung Moon. In reality it meant a lot of following rules, prayer and fasting. Not unlike the experience of most Christians who are active in their church. Biblically the full transformation that we call sanctification involves retraining oneself to listen to God, through the Holy Spirit, and not bad advice, bad habits, bad cultural models and so on. This transformation goes to the core of who we are and cannot be accomplished without the Holy Spirit of God, made available through Jesus Christ.

How does a Moonie draw closer to God? The Moonies deeply respect Jesus and his sacrifice, but at the center of their affections is Sun Myung Moon as the Lord of the Second Advent. Does the atonement, the sacrifice of Jesus on the cross, apply to them? Most of the Christians I know would say absolutely not. Moonies pray to God and love Jesus, but their trust is in Moon. On the other hand, they work very hard at changing their lifestyle, harder than most Christians that I know. As to whether or not this implies some sort of sanctification, I will let God judge. Certainly, a Moonie would say, "Yes."

Moonies practiced personal sacrifice which they called "indemnity" (DP 1973, 222-227). This was meant to fortify them against the guilt of sin. The Moonies do not use the term "works righteousness" because it is so clearly prohibited in scripture (Titus 3:5). Instead, they used the term indemnity, which is a legal or financial term indicating that a person has insured themselves against financial loss or legal responsibility. Reparations paid to the victor in war are called indemnity. In the church's use of the word, it was a personal sacrifice to secure God's protection from the responsibility for sin, either for the individual's sin or on behalf of someone else such as a relative (dead or alive), or even a nation.

In practice, indemnity in the Unification Church took the form of cold showers, fasting, or other forms of self-denial. Self-sacrifice has long been used among Christians to get God's attention. Lenten sacrifices are a common practice. And, we know that many monastic communities practice extreme self-sacrifice. The Moonies claimed that this atoned for sin in the same way that Old Testament sacrifices atoned for sin.

Since the Moonies do not believe in the full atonement on the cross, they instead substitute the "Blessing," which was the wedding ritual presided over by Moon himself with his wife,

Hak Ja Han, as "True Parents." Unification Church marriage was meant to attach the participant to the blood line of Sun Myung Moon. Since he believed himself to be sinless, that meant that the participant is now attached to the sinless bloodline of the *True Parents*. In theory, this eliminates the need for atonement from sin nature.

This is a quick snapshot of Moonie thinking as experienced during my time in the church. It should be clear that Unification theology does not line up with traditional Christianity. Moon himself called Unificationism a "younger brother" to Christianity. Moonies do use the same Bible and do engage with many current theological trends in the body of Christ. Moonies are intelligent and well educated. Moonies are often able to seriously undermine any Christian who is not either dogmatic in their theology or clear in their understanding of what it means to be a part of the body of Christ. I have never been in favor of dogmatism. The saying in seminary is that the seminary produces many atheists. This is precisely because the first thing a seminary does is to break through dogmatism, leaving the seminarian open to rethinking their Christianity.

The Practical Problem of Sin

For most Christians, all these questions about atonement, sanctification, and works may not seem to have much significance for their daily life. What does it mean for the Christian, or the Moonie, out on the street?

Unfortunately, like the three young men in the mall quoting "All have sinned..." (Romans 3:23), many if not most Christians function with an attitude that sin is our normal condition, so try to do better, but don't sweat it. Look down the page from the above quote from Romans 3, "he had passed over former sins" (*Romans 3:25*). You are forgiven, now go and "sin no more" (*John 5:14 &*

8:11). As Romans 6 states, we are not supposed to keep sinning after our former sins have been dealt with.

I know that born again, Spirit filled Christians sin, and that there is forgiveness for those sins. What I am pointing to is a shallowness of faith that accepts sin as a normal part of Christian life. I used this approach several times, always with the same result. These young men walked away, unable to answer Romans 6. There is an answer.

The answer is the Spirit of the living God. The spiritual voice of the first Great Awakening, Jonathan Edwards, states that the reason that Jesus came and sacrificed himself was so that we could know the Holy Spirit:

> The sum of the blessings Christ sought, by what
> he did and suffered in the work of redemption was
> the Holy Spirit (Edwards 2004, 55).

It is our communion with the Holy Spirit which transforms our lives. Most Christians know that tug in the gut that discourages us from doing things which didn't seem to bother us before we gave our lives to Christ. When we cooperate with that "still, small voice" *(1Kings 19:12, KJV)* we find that our lifestyle changes, our attitudes change. The change is visible to all who know us.

Ligonier Ministries and LifeWay Research's recent State of Theology study seems to indicate that most Christians are unwitting heretics. In response to a recent survey published in *Christianity Today* under the title "Our Favorite Heresies of 2018" (Lindgren and Lee 2018), professor Timothy Larsen of Wheaton College says, "One discouragement was that regular churchgoers were *more* likely to deny the personhood of the Holy Spirit. Many churches are doing a poor job of teaching pneumatology." Professor Fred Sanders of Biola University suggests, "what is at work in many Christians is 'zeal without knowledge.'"

John Stackhouse of Crandall University sounds an even more ominous note, "The survey sounds a legitimate and important warning. If people fundamentally misunderstand basic Christian theology, they cannot convert to it or practice it but instead will be literally following a different religion." "Another very discouraging aspect of the survey is that a majority of responses agree the Holy Spirit is an impersonal force and most people are good by nature. If most people are good, why do they need salvation?" adds Sung Wook Chung, professor of Christian theology, at Denver Seminary.

It would seem that many, if not most, Christians belong to Christian culture, or the Christian club, but don't understand what it means to belong to Jesus Christ. They are taught who the enemies are (cults, the perverse, those who persecute Christians), but don't know the voice of the one who is the head of the church.

Listen to Jonathan Edwards describe Christians who have been converted by emotional preaching, but not the Spirit:

> When they first were stirred by a legalistic fear of hell, they may have worried about the appearance of the evil in their lives, but after a while, having received this and that warm impression, they become convinced that they are justified to have a high opinion of themselves. Since they are no longer worried about hell. They neglect duties that are troublesome and inconvenient. If something in the Bible seems difficult or if it seems to require too much effort and pain, they ignore it, while at the same time they rationalize that various selfish pleasures are harmless.
>
> Instead of embracing Christ as their Savior from sin, these people are actually trusting in Him to help them save their sin. Instead of flying to Him as their refuge from their spiritual enemies, they

use Him to defend themselves against God. They
turn Christ into the devil's helper, so that they
may comfortably continue to sin against God,
assuming that Christ will protect them from
God's judgment (Edwards 1999, 245).

My brief meeting with the young men at the mall would
certainly not allow me to make judgments about their lifestyle.
My point is that although these young men were quick to rush
in to get someone saved, they were completely unable to answer
some of the fundamentals of scripture. As far as I could tell, their
complete understanding of Christianity amounted to a few Bible
quotes and the "four spiritual laws." They wanted to get me saved
but likely had no idea of what exactly they were saving me from.

These three young men set upon me smug in their salvation,
but left bewildered and confused. On the other hand, as a faithful
Moonie at the time, I left with my smugness intact and well-polished.

Not So Perfect

The Unification Church's morals were very conservative. They
were similar to those of conservative Christians. This included no
alcohol or cigarettes, no foul language, and it especially meant no
sexual misconduct. Premarital sex, homosexuality, or other sexual
misdeeds were considered the worst sins for the reasons stated
earlier. Unification Church teaching was that the fall of man in
the second chapter of Genesis was actually sexual sin. In essence,
the "apple" in the garden was unlawful sex. Once a person was a
church member, sexual sins were considered close to unforgivable.

After several years in the church, I had more free time, more
freedom of movement and my own sleeping quarters. This also
meant that I and other like-minded friends who did not think
having a beer or two was wrong could slip away to a relaxing

evening away having a few drinks where the eyes of judgment couldn't see us. I do not agree with those who suggest that alcohol is sinful and should not be consumed by Christians. This would put me in league with those who accused Christ of being a drunkard (Matthew 11:19; Luke 7:34). Scripture does condemn drunkards, habitual alcohol abusers (Deuteronomy 21:20-21; 1 Corinthians 5:11). But, Jesus and the disciples all consumed alcohol.

In any case, my friends and I didn't see anything particularly wrong with enjoying time apart from the strict rules. Living the image of perfection can be stressful after a number of years. I suppose if we were truly brainwashed it wouldn't be so hard.

More troubling are the accusations of Nansook Hong, who was the wife of Moon's eldest son, Hyo Jin Moon by Hak Ja Han, Moon's second or third wife, depending on who you asked. In Hong's autobiographical book *The Shadow of the Moons: My Life in the Reverend Sun Myung Moon's Family* (Hong 1998), she outlines a rather imperfect "True Family," leading to her decision to take her five children and flee her husband Hyo Jin Moon. She claimed he was abusive and a drug addict.

Hyo Jin was still a teenager during my time at the seminary. As the eldest son of the "True Family," he had the position of heir apparent for leadership of the church. He would visit the seminary often with the son of Moon's right-hand man, Bo Hi Pak, who was of similar age. The two were wild and undisciplined. I remember the two running through the student lounge flinging food raided from the food pantry. When the president of the seminary, David Kim, knew that they were coming, he would hide all the archery equipment and guns used for target practice. He was concerned for their safety and the safety of anyone near them. By this time, Hyo Jin had already been expelled from two boarding schools. The scuttlebutt was that he had been expelled from the last one for climbing a tree and shooting passersby with a BB gun.

The seminary was on a large acreage next to the Hudson River. On one occasion, Hyo Jin and the younger Pak had been out on the nearby lagoon with others in rowboats. It seems that the horseplay got too exuberant, and the teenage son of a couple who served on staff at the seminary was lost overboard. His body was not recovered until several days later, after an exhaustive search. Many of the seminarians were involved in the search for the body.

Hong's marriage to Hyo Jin came after my time in the church. Her accusations revealed in the book or in the CBS news interview, available on the internet, seem very plausible. According to Hong, who seems intelligent and sensible, Sun Myung Moon had numerous sexual affairs, unacceptable by church teaching, but which he excused because of his position as the new Christ. Exactly how she knows this, I am not sure.

A number of events in the last several decades since my time in the church have not put the best light on the "True Family." There have been power struggles, changes in leadership and several sons and daughters have left the church. As mentioned earlier, one son has created his own new church of heavily armed followers. He himself wears a crown composed of bullets. The idea of a sinless bloodline would appear to be ridiculous.

It is hard to know exactly what is true and what is not, but one thing is perfectly clear. The "True Parents" and the "True Family" are definitely not perfect. By all accounts, they are as dysfunctional, if not more so, as any other family you and I are likely to encounter. Any claim to spiritual ascendancy over and above Jesus is ridiculous fantasy.

My Own Encounter with a Moonie

I had been out of the Unification Church many years and was now a committed Christian having a late dinner with friends after church when a Moonie fundraiser walked into the restaurant with a box of candy. His name tag led me to quiz him about his father, who turned out to have been one of my classmates at

Unification Theological Seminary. He was eager to keep moving, but we delayed him long enough to quiz him a bit.

You see, the fundraiser was the child of a "blessed" couple, that is, a couple married by the "True Parents," and therefore a partaker in the theoretical bloodline of Sun Myung Moon. The question of atonement was back in play. My natural question was the same as it was with the fundamentalists, "Do you sin?" He was not comfortable giving an honest answer, so I pressed the issue, "You, as a child of the *Blessing*, should be sinless. Are you?" He turned and fled back into the night.

I genuinely wish he had stayed and conversed with us more. If Moon is not able to effect any genuine change to the human condition, then his claim to be the second coming of Christ is foolish. Moon himself said as much in one of his "Master Speaks" talks, which I recorded in one of my journals. Although an overeager pastor had me dump all of my notes from my time as a Moonie, my recollection of what he said was, "If I do not establish the Kingdom of Heaven on Earth, I am not the Messiah."

Of course, I had a strong leg up when conversing with this young acolyte. I knew Moonie doctrine, and in this case, I even knew this young man's father. On the other hand, in this young man's eyes, I was an apostate member and therefore no longer redeemable. In the long run, clever arguments do not create new Christians. However, clever arguments may cause non-believers or even casual Christians to doubt themselves. The belief in what is bringing us to perfection (sanctification) is important. If supposed sanctification is not happening, then is it not time to revisit the fundamental belief behind it?

Moonies and the Christian Experience

Moon claimed that Jesus had come to him on a hillside in Korea when he was still a teenager. According to Moon, Jesus had instructed him to finish the work that He had started. I have no way to test the veracity of Moon's claim, so I take it at face value. As far as that goes, I don't see a big problem. Even the apostle Paul says, "Now I rejoice in my sufferings for your sake, and in my flesh, I am filling up what is lacking in Christ's afflictions for the sake of his body, that is, the church" (Colossians 1:24).

Paul is very clear that the work of Christ is finished in the sense that the power of God was released at the cross of Christ's crucifixion for our complete salvation, "For the message of the cross is foolishness to those who are perishing, but to us who are being saved it is the power of God" (1 Corinthians 1:18). What is incomplete is the application. Not everyone has allowed the power of God to work in their lives. "For all who are led by the Spirit of God are sons of God" (Romans 8:14). And, those who are not led of the Spirit still need to take the hand of the man who stilled the waters.

It appears that Moon's childhood experience got twisted over the years. He was born in what is now North Korea. His parents converted to Christianity when he was a child, so he was raised in the Presbyterian Church. In his twenties, he spent time in a church led by messianic minister Baek Moon Kim, spreading the message of the "New Israel." It would seem that this teaching had a great deal to do with reshaping Moon's understanding of the gospel.

In any case, the enthusiasm of Moon and his followers for creating heaven on earth is certainly laudable. Clearly this has its roots in the Christian message. While much of the gospel points to a glorious future with Christ, that future kingdom is based on the transformation of ourselves into fully realized sons and daughters of God, people who act and think differently from others. The result of this transformation is a different sort of world, a world filled with mercy, a world which reflects heaven here on earth. Hospitals, orphanages, a social safety net, public schools and libraries are all a good start, but they are not the finished product.

If we reflect back to Daniel Day Williams' definition of liberal theology: "It is that form of Christian faith in which a prophetic-progressive philosophy of history culminates in the expectation of the coming of the Kingdom of God on earth." We can see that it is entirely possible that Moon in his Presbyterian roots would have already been primed for this.

I also grew up Presbyterian. Like many mainline churches, the church of my parents still respected the traditions, in this case the Westminster Confession of Faith. In practice, the preaching seemed softened toward the agenda of the theological liberals. As a result, despite Moon pushing the boundary further than any of the liberal theologians would dare, the teaching didn't seem all that strange to me.

I think the issue is that much of Christian thought and certainly Moon's approach is based on pushing ourselves to the limit to create a better world. That certainly isn't a bad thing, but how is that any different than any other well intended non-Christian who is trying to create a better world?

CHAPTER EIGHT

THE SOCIAL GOSPEL

Your Kingdom Come

"Your will be done, on earth as it is in heaven" (Matthew 6:10). This was the rallying cry of the Social Gospel movement; whose chief figures Washington Gladden and Walter Rauschenbusch were both liberal theologians. Both men died in 1918, and the movement lost steam after that, probably due more to the after-effects of World War I than anything else.

Karl Barth took up the critique of the social gospel, pointing out that the movement lacked sufficient understanding of the depth of human sinfulness. By my time in seminary, Paul Tillich, and more particularly H. Richard Niebuhr and Reinhold Niebuhr (Richard's older brother), had all developed Barth's *neo-orthodox* response, calling for a social gospel built on a deep biblical faith, which was more comfortable for conservative Christians.

Harvey Cox appears to revert to a social gospel message which Richard Niebuhr sums up as, "A God without wrath brought men without sin into a kingdom without judgment through the ministrations of a Christ without a cross" (Niebuhr, H. Richard 1959). The Moonies also believe that sin was a significant but manageable issue, that is, Moon did not believe the cross was necessary to overcome sin nature. Instead, he had substituted a life of indemnification, what could be referred to as *white knuckle religion*, that is, keep trying harder and making greater sacrifices until you get to your perfection. This of course was added to submission to the sinless blood line of Sun Myung Moon. We have already cast aside the idea that Moon's bloodline is sinless, which rejects its usefulness in creating a sinless race to inhabit a new kingdom of God on earth as in heaven.

Dietrich Bonhoeffer in letters to a friend speaks of a world that is moving to secularization, a time without religion:

> What is bothering me incessantly is the question what Christianity really is, or indeed who Christ really is, for us today. The time when people could be told everything by means of words, whether theological or pious, is over, and so is the time of inwardness and conscience—and that means the time of religion in general. We are moving towards a completely religionless time; people as they are now simply cannot be religious any more (Bonhoeffer 1967, 139).

It should be understood that these are not finished thoughts, but musings sent to a good friend from a Nazi prison cell. Since Cox refers to Bonhoeffer as his inspiration, we should take a deeper look at Bonhoeffer and his understanding of secularization and the future with Christ. I have loved Bonhoeffer's writing since first reading *The Cost of Discipleship* (Bonhoeffer 1959). We will see that Cox and Bonhoeffer are not seeing things the same way.

The Ultimate and the Penultimate

Writing from prison in 1944, with just less than a year before his hanging by the Nazis, Bonhoeffer is writing of a religionless time. At the same time, he was still working on his book *Ethics* (Bonhoeffer 1955), which was never completed. *Ethics* was published never-the-less with what Bonhoeffer had finished and with those notes that could be recovered. It gives a much deeper insight into his thoughts on secularism and society without religion.

For him, the loss of the unity of the West under religion and government is dissolving under the onslaught of technology, which released a revolt of the masses calling for a defiant nationalism:

> The millions who possessed and could posses no other title of nobility than their own undeserved wretchedness now raised their accusation and their claim against both the nobility of blood and the nobility of achievement. The masses have equal contempt for the laws of blood and for the laws of reason. They make their own law, the law of misery. It is a violent law, and short-lived. We today are standing at the culmination and crisis of this uprising (Bonhoeffer 1955, 100-102).

Remember, this is being written at a time when Fascism and Communism both have reached their zenith. A few pages later he writes, "The west is becoming hostile towards Christ" (Bonhoeffer 1955, 109). Bonhoeffer is not celebrating this end of religion, as Cox does. He sees the end of the outward display of religion in the West as allowing for a turn against Christ, the center and purpose for the Christian religion, and the center and purpose for humankind.

Bonhoeffer goes on to discuss the purpose of humankind; that is, the union of God's beloved with Christ and therefore with God the Father: "The origin and the essence of all Christian life are comprised in the one process or event which the Reformation called justification of the sinner by grace alone" (Bonhoeffer

1955, 120). This is, for Bonhoeffer, the last word, or the *ultimate* purpose, but the ultimate end must be reached by the step before the ultimate, the *penultimate*. This last step of the journey is essential to the end of the journey, but meaningless outside of the intended destination. Bonhoeffer sees all the good things that we desire, all those things encompassed by the social gospel, as important desires, but not essential to the ultimate goal. In opposition to Cox, Bonhoeffer says, "The preparation of the way for Christ cannot... be simply the realization of a program of social reform" (Bonhoeffer 1955, 137).

Christ in the World

All Kingdom minded theology starts with a world firmly in the grip of Christ. If nothing else, the Unification Church is Kingdom-minded. The Moonie's Christ is Sun Myung Moon, which sets the Moonie firmly outside of Christianity. The Moonie stands at odds with the meaning of the incarnation, the crucifixion, and the resurrection. In the preceding chapter, I dealt with the Unificationist understanding of Christ and their alternate view of the crucifixion. Because the Unificationist view is that Jesus' mission ended in failure requiring a second coming of Christ to finish the unfinished work, it should not be a surprise that the Unification view of the resurrection is significantly depleted. Jesus returned after the resurrection to help his followers prepare for a second coming. In the Unificationist view, Jesus was trying to get the church ready to receive a second Christ. This is definitely not the Christian view: "The deed of God is Jesus Christ, a reconciliation" (Bonhoeffer 1955, 55).

As we just saw, Bonhoeffer places the central core of the work of Christ, and therefore his Church, in "justification by grace." The more complete Reformation statement is, "justification by grace through faith alone." The word "faith" has become a dogmatic assertion in some Christian circles, and the meaning is sometimes blurred. It can be used as a blunt object to mean to believe, but exactly what believing means is not always clear. It might be better to use the term confidence (*con fidere*): we are justified by confidence, our confidence in our relationship to Christ Jesus. That confidence comes from knowing him, from having him close enough to us that we hear his voice whispering to us.

By this standard, the Moonies had no confidence in Jesus. Their confidence was in works of penance (indemnity) under the direction of Sun Myung Moon. The Unification Church was an environment with a heavy control structure intended to keep the Moonies righteous. As I stated earlier, the rules resembled those of many conservative Christian denominations: no drinking, no smoking, no sex outside of marriage, no foul language and so on.

I opened this book with the story of a breakfast meeting where one of the pastors present asked me why I became a Moonie. At that same breakfast, an older woman, who is a friend and who had recently become a Christian, leaned over to me and asked, "How do you know that God is real?" I described the relationship that I have with God now as a dance. I talk to God. I ask for directions, ask for help, or just ask for His presence. Then, God answers me back, and I get confidence in what I should be doing; problems resolve themselves, and I feel the presence of God. When I go back to talk to God, I am even more convinced of His reality. The more convinced I am, the more I talk to Him, and the more He comes to me or intervenes in my life. A dance seems the best way to describe it.

Recently, this same woman began describing several situations in her life. She described small miracles in answer to problems and issues she had struggled with and had asked God about. It immediately occurred to me, she was in the dance. Clearly, she was enjoying every minute of it.

Many denominations and many Christians function by rules. Some of the rules are nearly identical to those of the Unification

Church. As Bonhoeffer notes, and I agree completely, this may be the way of much, if not most, of the church, but it is not the way of Jesus. The way of Jesus is the way of relationship through the Holy Spirit. Living by rules of conduct, judging ourselves and others as to the righteousness or lack of righteousness of our actions, is the way of the Pharisee. Christian judgments create Christian Pharisees.

Relationship with Jesus Christ and therefore with God creates confidence in God. That confidence is then manifested in knowing His will and doing His will. Doing God's will, we will see results.

> It was not the thought and the will that the Pharisee failed to unite, but precisely the hearing and the doing. For the hearer of the word who makes the hearing independent there is the saying 'the doer shall be blessed in his doing' (Jas. 1:25). The doer is here the man who simply knows of no other possible attitude to the word of God when he has heard it than to do it (Bonhoeffer 1955, 49).

Bonhoeffer's *Ethics* often seems like an abstract discussion. It is hard to grasp what it means in real life. So, let's boil it down to real life situations. For instance, I was at a gas station gassing up my car when I felt the urge to speak to and to pray for the man gassing up next to me. This is an actual situation that occurred a few months ago. I hesitated, thinking is that really God, or am I just imagining that based on all the evangelical teaching I've been hearing recently? He finished and left and I never talked to him. I was left with a sense of having failed to react to the still small voice. It wasn't my lack of desire to follow God, it was my incessant self-evaluation that crowded the path. There is no point to condemning myself. It may not have been the Lord. Bonhoeffer makes extremely clear; the purpose is to redirect us to the one who holds all things in his hand and away from ourselves (Matthew 11:27; Luke 10:22; John 3:35 & 13:3; Romans 11:36).

This brings up another of Bonhoeffer's points: there is no corner of the world that Christ Jesus does not own, that is not in Jesus' hand. Satan operates only where he is allowed by the hand of God. Therefore, all the world belongs to God. There is no sacred versus secular. God operates anywhere and everywhere. I have a prayer closet which helps me to hear God much better, but I am free to pray, to preach, to teach, and to minister on the street, in a restaurant, or at a party. I pray for atheists, witches, and sinners of all stripes. I even pray for Christians.

The End for Which God Created

We have seen that Richardson suggests that "salvation in Christ" is nothing but a reset to the state of humanity before the Fall. Richardson refers to our Sabbath rest in God. Clearly, Bonhoeffer is also envisioning something beyond the forgiveness of sin, including sin nature. For Bonhoeffer, this new state means a laying down of all judgments against ourselves or against others, and it means a complete trust that the word that comes from God to God's people is the right word and that word needs no evaluation. God's word only needs implementation. For Bonhoeffer, man in the state of grace is always moving closer to God.

Richardson's ultimate end or purpose for man relies heavily on Jonathan Edwards' *A Dissertation Concerning the End for Which God Created the World* (Edwards 1765). This essay rests on Edward's meticulous logic, as well as an enormous volume of biblical quotations, to demonstrate that the ultimate purpose of us all, a purpose restored through Jesus Christ, is to glorify God. We were created to glorify God and to receive our own glory in response to fulfilling that purpose (Romans 2:7). This understanding underlies Richardson's discussion of what it means to enter into God's Sabbath rest. In Edwards' terms, we achieve our happiest state when we are in our closest union with God, which is achieved when we bring glory to God. This state, which Richardson refers to as our Sabbath rest, accords well with Bonhoeffer's view of humanity's final purpose.

Shortly before his crucifixion, Jesus converses with a crowd of people. As told by John, in his gospel account, Jesus says, "Now is my soul troubled. And what shall I say? 'Father, save me from this hour?' But for this purpose I have come to this hour. Father, glorify your name" (John 12:27-28). God Himself responds, "I have glorified it, and I will glorify it again" (John 12:28). Edwards points to this as one of many instances where God's ultimate purpose is spelled out. Jesus does not say, "glorify my name," although many passages attach the glorification of Jesus and the glorification of the Father to his crucifixion, he says "glorify your name," subordinating himself to God's glorification. Moreover, God affirms the statement, showing an obvious pleasure in Jesus. The next verse indicates that God's response was clearly heard by all, even if some heard only thunder; others were convinced that an angel had spoken. Then, Jesus replies, "This voice has come for your sake, not mine. Now is the judgment of this world; now will the ruler of this world be cast out. And I, when I am lifted up from the earth, will draw all people to myself" (John 12:30-32).

There are several ways to interpret the phrase, "Now is the judgment of this world." It certainly doesn't mean the final judgment of the world. The most typical interpretation is that God's judgment is to be decided at the cross: "Now is approaching the decisive scene, the eventful period—the crisis—when it shall be determined who shall rule this world" (Barnes 1834). I think it should also be possible to read this statement as, "Now is the time when the world will judge." In this case, the world, and the Jewish leaders in particular, will judge Christ according to the temptations of Satan's accusations. Because Jesus Christ is the sinless incarnation, the judgment and murder by crucifixion of Jesus is an injustice of the highest proportion, far beyond blasphemy. This injustice takes from Satan and from humankind all rights, real or imagined, and places all things rightfully in the hands of Jesus Christ (John 13:3). Satan lost all his claims at the cross. He may be dangerous and destructive still, but he has lost all authority. Essentially, Satan is a homeless thief with a warrant on his head.

> Jesus Christ the crucified—this means that God pronounces its final condemnation on the fallen creation. The rejection of God on the cross of Jesus Christ contains within itself the rejection of the whole human race without exception. The cross of Jesus is the death sentence upon the world. Man cannot glory now in his humanity, nor the world in its divine orders. The glory of men has come now to its last end in the face of the Crucified, bruised and bloody and spat upon. Yet the crucifixion of Jesus does not simply mean the annihilation of the created world, but under this sign of death, the cross, men are now to continue to live, to their own condemnation if they despise it, but to their own salvation if they give it its due. The ultimate has become real in the cross, as the judgement upon all that is penultimate, yet also as mercy towards that penultimate which bows before the judgement of the ultimate (Bonhoeffer 1955, 131).

The ultimate, the final purpose of humanity and all of creation, is made manifest on the cross. Everything that stands prior to the ultimate, the penultimate, is under eternal condemnation. And yet, to all of humanity and to all of creation which bows before the judgment of God, there is mercy.

And so, Jesus says, "when I am lifted up from the earth, [I] will draw all people to myself" (John 12:32). Jesus has glorified God in all he has done, and so God will glorify Jesus in his Resurrection three days later. In the one simple statement, "I will draw all people to myself," Jesus is saying that the reconciliation between God and all of creation will be made real. Now, as we come to glorify Jesus, the Spirit of God is released, and his glorification will reach far beyond the perfunctory to a true intimacy.

Whether we approach this final or ultimate end by the glorification of Jesus, and therefore the Father as does Jonathan Edwards, or by bowing to the judgment of the cross as in Bonhoeffer, or by our Sabbath rest in Jesus as in Richardson, the end is essentially the same, a living union with God by our relationship with Jesus. All three of these approaches attack the root of the problem at its source, the Fall of Adam and Eve. Attacking the social issues, as Harvey Cox suggests, does not solve the real problem; it tries to heal the symptoms without healing the disease. Christianity has been at the forefront of dealing with social issues, but it has always maintained that the root of the problem was our relationship with God.

Christianity is meant to bring us to our penultimate step, but may easily step backwards into the deadness of the Pharisaical religion, as Tillich points out, "The Church, like all its members, relapses from the New into the Old Being" (Tillich 1955. 24). Tillich is telling us that Christianity fails if it does not bring us to a relationship with Jesus and God the Father through the Holy Spirit. Church culture, our doctrine, style, rules and so on, is of little importance to those who embrace the ultimate purpose, becoming a new person in Christ. "We should not be too worried about the Christian religion... This is circumcision; and the the lack of of it, the secularization which is spreading all over the world is uncircumcision. Both are nothing, of no importance, if the ultimate question is asked, the question of a New Reality" (Tillich 1955. 18-19).

Because the Unification Church started with a view of the Fall based on sexual misconduct, it is not surprising that their approach was chiefly to repair moral infrastructure. They advocate the necessity of placing all marriages under the bloodline of Moon. In the Unificationist view, it would no longer be possible for someone born into a sinless bloodline to sin (DP 1973, 100-102).

Let's imagine a child born into a world in which sin has been completely eliminated. Is that any different than Adam and Eve in the Garden of Eden? If Adam and Eve chose the knowledge of good and evil, what protects this new child from a similar choice? As we have seen, some of Moon's own children don't appear to be paragons of virtue even though the claim is that their bloodline is pure. So, the bloodline argument does not play well. However, what if that child is born into a world that embraces the Spirit of the Living God and submits all human wisdom to that light instead? What if the world of that child is fully submitted to God? This is the Kingdom of God.

Moonies celebrating the Washington Monument Rally in 1976. My friend and colleague Lee Shapiro in front center.

Colonel Bo Hi Pak, Moon's right-hand man, celebrating the Washington Monument Rally in 1976. Next to him in sunglasses is the then president of the Unification Church in the United States Neil Albert Salonen.

Moonies rally outside of the courthouse during Sun Myung Moon's trial for tax evasion. 1980-1982.

Another photo of the same rally including hundreds of Moonies and a brass band dressed in bright red uniforms.

This is the mass wedding of 2,000 couples held at Madison Square Gardens on July 1, 1982.

Sun Myung Moon blesses the couples as they pass in front of him.

"True Parents" sprinkling the couples with holy water as they pass between them, three couples at a time.

The Little Angels Folk Ballet. One of many performers who followed the wedding ceremony.

CHAPTER NINE

PRAYER

Praying to God

Everybody prays, or at least everybody rolls their thoughts around talking to whatever voice there is there in their head. It might be God. It might be their demons. It might be the split parts of their personality. It might actually be just talking to oneself. But, everybody does it. For a Christian, prayer should be the foundation of their faith. For Moonies, prayer was essential to daily life.

Moonies pray to God the Father, just like all Christians. There is one significant difference; even though they honor Jesus, when Moonies finish a prayer "in the name of your Son, our Lord," they don't mean Jesus, they mean Moon. Moonie prayer usually begins with bowing to the portrait of Moon and his wife, the *True Parents*. This often includes a pledge of loyalty.

In my experience, Moonies do not have a problem praying in the name of Jesus when they are sitting side by side with proper Christians. They have an extreme respect and honor for Jesus, even if they don't believe him to be God incarnate. As a Moonie, I would stop in Catholic churches to pray, since they were more likely to be open during the day. Most Catholic churches have a very large crucifix at the front of the sanctuary. Looking up at the crucifix would cause me to meditate on the suffering and sacrifice of Jesus. I sometimes felt this to be almost overwhelming.

Remember that Moonies, with their heretical Christology, do not believe in the atonement as normal Christians do. Their understanding of the resurrection is also limited. And their understanding of the role of the Holy Spirit is limited as well. And so, the Moonie understanding of Christ as the head of His church is largely symbolic. The result is a focus on the sacrifice and suffering of Jesus, ignoring the victory of Jesus as outlined in scripture. The Unificationist understanding of Jesus stops with his sacrificing himself on the cross. There is no meaningful understanding of the resurrection, though there is a great deal of empathy for Christ's sacrifice.

Moonie prayer

Corporate prayer was a big deal for the Moonies. But, individual prayer was also emphasized. I grew up with the staged corporate prayer of the Presbyterians. It was often written ahead of time and read. At meals, we usually had the quick prayer, which in our home was referred to as "saying grace." None of it felt deep, earnest, or particularly heart-felt. I don't want to denigrate the prayer of the Presbyterians; my inability to engage deeply was as much because I was unable to see God in that prayer setting as anything else. Unfortunately, I know far too many men and women who were dragged to church constantly as children but who have never felt the touch that comes from deep personal prayer. It is a shame that someone could spend years in Christian community but never engage with Jesus or the Holy Spirit.

Prayer was essential for the Moonies. Every center I was in had a room set aside for prayer. In larger centers, there would be a large gathering area for corporate prayer and sometimes a smaller room for private prayer or study. Gathering for an hour of corporate prayer was the standard beginning to the day at every Unification Church center.

While the Moonies occasionally do engage in corporate prayer as most know it in the West, individuals praying aloud, one after the other. Corporate prayer at Moonie centers normally involved everyone present in the center gathering to pray personally, out loud, and all at once. It was energetic, but not terribly comprehensible to an outside observer. As I understand, this is the style of corporate prayer practiced by most Korean Christians. Through that, I learned to pray with intensity. I learned to address God the Father directly and know that I was talking to Him. My prayer wasn't a corporate statement, since it was unlikely my personal cry to God would have been picked out from the din of voices by anyone else but God. Our gathering together to pray, all at once, was its own corporate statement. I learned to make prayer a daily habit.

That same intensity carried over into my private prayer life. The seminary was the place that afforded me the most time for private prayer. Before bed, I would usually retire to the chapel and pray, either kneeling or lying face down with arms extended (cruciform). The hard and cold slate of the chapel floor helped to keep me awake at the end of a long day when my zeal was fading.

My favorite place to pray, however, was a secluded spot in the woods. The seminary had several wooded acres. My spot had a huge rock face jutting out of a steep hillside deep in the woods. I would climb to the top and sit there to pour out my heart to heaven. I have learned that where you pray makes a difference. That isn't to say you shouldn't pray whenever and wherever you are. But, if there is a place that you feel closer to God, that is the best place to pray. That can be a room set aside for prayer, it can be nothing more than a favorite chair, or it can be a secret place in the woods. I never took anyone else to my special spot in the woods. It was my own place to be alone with God.

I have always felt closer to God and heaven when I am alone in nature. Now days, I like to spend time in the morning sitting on my patio, which faces Galveston Bay. I read my Bible, I listen to God, and I pray. I especially like to take my kayak to Armand Bayou, a nearby nature preserve. It covers many acres of natural wetlands in the heart of the greater Houston area. I feel the presence of God there more intensely. In the wonder of God's incredible creation, I don't really feel the need to speak. Rather, I enjoy drinking in His presence. To me, it is a real privilege to be allowed to paddle my kayak in a place so close to home and yet relatively unmarked by human hands.

The Cry for Help

While a Moonie in England, I had an English friend who I'll called Ed for our purposes. Ed was a Christian. I'll talk more about Ed in another chapter. When Ed and I prayed, Ed started with a self-centered, self-interested prayer: a bigger house, a better job, more money. I prayed in the manner of a Moonie. I started with honoring the great and painful sacrifice of Jesus, not in a perfunctory manner, but fervently. I then went on to pray for England, for the moral climate of England, for the health of the church, for wisdom in Parliament, and so on. Because Moonies saw themselves in a sacrificial role, it was not normal for a Moonie to pray for themselves. I did not pray for any personal needs.

For Ed, this was a wake-up call. Christians fall easily into complacency unless there is someone or something to keep them stirred up. We don't naturally remember to stir ourselves up and must be reminded (2 Peter 1:13). In this case, I was Ed's reminder. As his pastor demonstrated in a meeting I attended at Ed's church, the pastor was less interested in praying for wisdom and more interested in fuming about cults. And, as we have seen, Ed was wrapped up in his own concerns. (To my view, Ed didn't need a bigger house, he needed someone to share his house with.) Much of Ed's problem, and the problem of many Christians, was a lack of doing what Jesus calls us to do: "love your neighbor as yourself" (Matthew 19:19 & 22:39; Mark 12:31). Loving is an art and a skill. It is honed by hard work and effort. There are a lot of ways to love, but it all starts with praying for someone other than yourself. When you do that, it is amazing how much smaller your problems seem to become. After hearing my "Moonie" prayer, Ed asked if he could pray again.

The Calling of Christ

The calling of Christ is not to finger-pointing or complaining. It is not to that of waving placards on the street corner. The first deacons were selected so that the Apostles could, as Peter says, "devote ourselves to prayer and to the ministry of the word" (Acts 6:4). Prayer is essential for a healthy church.

The Lord's prayer is our model (Matthew 6:9-13; Luke 11:2-4). I use the Lord's prayer as an outline; I don't think it was intended to be the prayer that we pray repeatedly on Sunday morning. At the same time, it is good to pray it often just to remind ourselves of the standard for prayer. This prayer starts with honoring God. Honoring God is worship. "Our Father who art in heaven," is a simple heart-felt statement of worship. Worship could be an hour of singing and making music to God, or it could be time on my face before God. As a charismatic Christian, I spend a lot of time in praise. I see it as foundational to prayer. This was a weak spot for the Moonies. Their vision was so thoroughly Kingdom-minded that they moved almost immediately to the Lord's Prayer, part two, and parked there. The Moonies do sing a lot, but their songs are less worship and more, "If I had a hammer..."

Jesus' part two is praying for the Father's kingdom to come on earth as in heaven. God's kingdom does not include corruption, or perversion, and it doesn't include bickering and fighting. Pray for wisdom. Pray for godliness. Pray for peace in government institutions. Pray for justice in the judicial system. Pray for honest wealth in the economy so that all hard work is well rewarded and there is plenty left over to help the poor or the indigent. Pray for the hospitals and the schools. Pray for generosity. Pray for humility. These are all at the core of Moonie prayer. How much more should these be an important part of prayer for all Christians.

Only then does Jesus' prayer move to the personal level. It is definitely acceptable to pray for your personal needs. Don't forget to pray for God's protection from temptation, from lust, from unwise thoughts. I used to have bad dreams at night. I learned that if I asked God to protect my thoughts as I slept just before I went to sleep, I didn't have bad dreams.

Spirit Led Prayer

Prayer has been a special passion of mine since I was asked to lead a Sunday morning hour of prayer many years ago. In some ways, I would say that the Moonie passion for prayer informed me, but there are several ways that Moonie patterns worked against prayer as it is meant to be practiced in the Christian context.

In seminary, I had instruction in *pneumatology*, the study of the Holy Spirit. It has been a long time since those days, and I can say now confidently that I do not believe my professor had much firsthand knowledge of the Holy Spirit. Neither did the Moonies know the presence of the Holy Spirit, for reasons which I hope are obvious. As energetic and heart-felt as Moonie prayer was, it lacked one important ingredient: the Holy Spirit. We prayed with the very best of intentions, with all of the wisdom we could muster, and with all the loving and the caring we had in us, but lacking the wisdom of God's direction, we are bound by the limits of our own soul.

the Spirit helps us in our weakness. For we do not
know what to pray for as we ought, but the Spirit
himself intercedes for us with groanings too deep
for words (Romans 8:26).

Experience tells me that when I am in prayer and I feel an
urging to pray for something odd, I need to follow that urging.
That "still small voice" is usually the Holy Spirit, and typically
the results are a level of prayer intensity that is surprising to me
at the time. Often, the prayer is directed to something entirely off
my radar and which I normally have no particularly deep feeling
about. I have to say that the intensity is not my own. This is clearly
the Holy Spirit prompting me what to pray and energizing that
prayer. This has happened both in individual prayer times and
praying together with other Christians who are familiar with the
Holy Spirit. It never happened to me as a Moonie.

Prayer that engages the Holy Spirit and prayer that is instigated
by the Holy Spirit will always trump the prayer of my momentary
desire, no matter how loving and heart-felt. For the Spirit-filled
Christian, prayer is the most important and powerful weapon
available. The Holy Spirit prompts us what to pray and when to
pray and carries our prayers to the throne of heaven. But what
about the prayers of those like the Moonies who don't have the
Holy Spirit and may not even know Jesus?

CHAPTER TEN

PRAYER AND WITCHCRAFT

Visualize World Peace

The popular bumper sticker "Visualize World Peace" was created as a response to Sri Chinmoy's call to visualize peace, or at least that is how I recall the matter. Sri Chinmoy is a Hindu teacher who was particularly popular in the 1970's and early 1980's. The "visualization" referred to in the bumper sticker is actually a form of prayer which relies on fixing the image of the desired goal in the mind. In that sense, it is not unlike repetitive prayers.

I am not a fan of repetitive prayer. It is too easy for such rote prayers to become an exercise done without heart or clear direction (Matthew 6:7). In fact, it can become little more than a personal statement of superiority. A study from Colorado State University suggests that drivers with bumper stickers that announce their beliefs are more aggressive and more easily irritated. It doesn't seem to matter if the statement is peace and love, "visualize whirled peas" or a Darwin fish.

I have been to auto dealer auctions with a friend who points out other dealers who have used him in an unethical manner.

One such individual wears prayer beads and his daughter wears a hijab. Jesus says, "And when you pray, you must not be like the hypocrites. For they love to stand and pray in the synagogues and at the street corners, that they may be seen by others. Truly, I say to you, they have received their reward" (Matthew 6:5). Prayers made as a public statement may have their weight in public opinion, but not in God's opinion.

The other element here, for a committed Christian, is the question that this raises of non-Christian prayer. All religions worship or pray. Does God not hear and answer their prayer? My answer is yes and no. If the prayer is addressed to God, He surely hears it. If you are a friend of God, or desperately desire to be a friend of God, then you will have a better idea of how to talk to God and get a positive answer. If you are distant from God and ask for things that God doesn't want for you, you may or may not get an answer. Or you may not get the answer you are looking for.

What about a Hindu, an animist, a Satanist or Wiccan who prays to something other than God? Obviously, if you are asking Satan for something, you are asking Satan for an answer, not God. It gets trickier if the prayer or visualization or whatever is not addressed to anyone in particular. This is the case for instance with Buddhism in which the "Godhead" is not seen as personal. Like the Star Wars "Force," there is no one to answer.

Spiritual Mechanisms

There are several ways to look at prayer that is not addressed specifically to anyone. Buddhists have two main objectives in prayer. One is to concentrate the mind on the desired result. The second is to send blessings out to the universe, to people, to other created beings, etc. There is no question that the Bible puts great stock in both blessings and curses. A man or a woman who blesses or curses is sending energy for or against someone, and the Bible takes that seriously (Psalm 109:17). What God blesses or curses will clearly override any other blessing or curse (Psalm 109:28). So if you ask me if prayers not addressed to God but thrown out to the atmosphere or some other deity have an effect, I would have to answer yes. In essence, we are discussing mechanisms designed to apply spiritual force to achieve a desired result, be it good or bad.

Spiritual mechanisms which lie outside of prayer as practiced by most Christians include mind concentration, mind control, self-hypnosis, hypnosis or any other technique for channeling thoughts and feelings. The most common is mental concentration. These may have useful purposes, but they are not prayer. These all rely on using the hidden resources of the mind to accomplish a goal. There are plenty of people who claim expertise in these various methods, but the inner reaches of the mind are not well understood. Meddling in these regions can have unforeseen results. Applied to anyone other than yourself, these techniques can be dangerous and unethical. Any time someone is attempting to change the mind, the will or the physical state of another person through mental concentration, psychic manipulation, spells or curses, this falls under the heading of witchcraft. Even some prayer can be witchcraft in disguise. The bottom line: is God being called on or activated, in accordance with the will of heaven, or is my will being enforced against someone else's will?

Witchcraft

The Unification Church crossed several lines forbidden by the Bible. One of the most significant is necromancy, contacting the dead. Saul, the first king of Israel, used the witch of En-dor to raise the spirit of Samuel for him. God had passed over several of Saul's shortcomings, but this one brought an immediate response. Samuel, speaking through the medium, let Saul know he would die in battle the next day along with his sons (I Samuel 28), and so it was (I Samuel 31:2-4). Sun Myung Moon had no qualms about contacting the dead. He had several sittings with the American spiritualist Arthur Ford. Moonies were often familiar with many occult and spiritualist thinkers, including Madame Blavatsky and Theosophy, Emanuel Swedenborg, Edgar Cayce and others.

While I was in the Unification Church, I had in my possession a transcript of a séance or psychic reading by Arthur Ford with Sun Myung Moon. Arthur Ford is the same spiritualist medium who conducted the séance to raise the spirit of Houdini on national radio. The Moonies were familiar with the Swedenborgian Church, which bases its thought on the Swedish Lutheran pastor Emanuel Swedenborg (1688-1772), known for his various writings on occult knowledge.

While I never saw any direct use of the occult during my time in the Unification Church outside of references to numerology, which were frequent, it is clear that talking to the dead was not condemned by the church. I am not aware of the Moonies themselves conducting a séance or in any other way attempting to contact the dead.

Many of the church members were familiar with other forms of occultism such as palm reading, card reading, astrology and numerology. These practices were not encouraged, but were certainly not discouraged either. Outside of numerology, I rarely saw any of these things practiced. None of the Moonies seemed expert in numerology, but a discussion of the significance of numbers was part of the church teaching and would be mentioned frequently when discussing daily events. Fasts often would be done for specific numbers of days: three, seven or twenty-one-day fasts were the most common. Numbers play a big part in the *Divine Principle* discussion of the History of Providence and Providential Time-Identity (DP 1973, 403).

New age and oriental medicine was also practiced. An acupuncturist was on staff at the seminary for a time. He had recently immigrated and was still perfecting his English, and I would guess was getting his licenses in order before opening a practice in the United States. The seminary also had a homeopathic physician on staff during my time there. I don't know that I would necessarily accuse either of these two practices of being occult, but I do know Christians who want nothing to do with either for spiritual reasons. The Unificationist approach was very open to new practices such as these; remember this was the late seventies when these practices were still considered exotic.

Although it was not common to do so, the Unification Church did incorporate some Korean folk practices on occasion. In an incident previously described, the son of a couple on staff at the seminary drowned while horse-playing with Moon's son and other teenagers. Several of the staff and seminarians were drafted to search the lagoon until the body was recovered.

An elderly Korean woman known for extraordinary visions and a practitioner of Korean folk arts, what we might call a witch doctor, was brought in. She was referred to as Lady Doctor Kim. A fire was built by the water's edge. Prayers were said. Those who had contact with the body were then asked to jump through the smoke. I believe the intention was to keep the spirit of the dead from clinging to the living.

While this sort of folk magic was uncommon in the church, it does point out that under the basically Christian culture of the Unification Church, there were a large number of beliefs that were essentially pagan or new age. This was evident especially in beliefs about the dead.

The *Divine Principle* teaches that the departed come back in spirit to help others advance spiritually. In this way, they themselves gain the same benefits of spiritual growth as the physical people they are helping (DP 1973, 185).

The church also believed in the power of mental projection or mind concentration. This is most commonly encountered in goal setting, especially for sales people. It was at the heart of Moonie fundraising.

The Fundraiser

One of the most important activities of the church was fundraising. It takes a lot of money to carry out large international evangelistic campaigns or to buy landmark properties. Fund raising was hard work. It involved pounding the pavement from early morning until well past dark. Most Moonies in those days were required to spend time fundraising. Everyone knew it was hard work. Those of us, like myself, who were not particularly outgoing, didn't really enjoy fundraising. It meant confronting strangers all day long and asking them to part with their hard-earned cash.

There were a few individuals who excelled at fundraising. One of the most well-known individuals in the church could bring home as much as two thousand dollars a day selling candy or flowers on the street corner. Remember, this was the late seventies, so that was a lot of money. While I had never met this individual, I did know who he was. As it happened, I stepped onto an elevator with him at a large hotel in downtown Manhattan which was owned by the church. As we were traveling up, neither one of us spoke or really acknowledged each other, but I suddenly had this overwhelming urge to reach into my pocket and give him my little bit of cash. Clearly this young man had mastered the ability to concentrate his thoughts far beyond that of prayer, but to that of hypnotic power. Moreover, since he was retiring for the night and not fundraising, he certainly had no reason to ask a fellow member for donations; it is hard not to think that his concentration on the goal had taken hold of him.

What is clear is that God does not allow us to force anyone to do something against their will, especially not through clandestine means. God is also clear that gaining knowledge through necromancy, psychics or other means outside of what is provided by the Holy Spirit is forbidden. This not only includes witchcraft, but also includes gossip, bribery and other practices which would insult strict justice. While I know that there are

"Christian" witches, "Christian" psychics and others who practice things forbidden by the Bible, I believe that calling themselves Christian and using Christian sounding language does not make them Christian (Matthew 7:21-23). This is not to encourage heresy hunters either. Jesus gives us the parable of the wheat and tares (Matthew 13:24-30) to discourage us from conducting witch hunts.

Remember that the law is our schoolmaster or guardian (Galatians 3:24-25). In other words, injunctions against witchcraft and the like are meant to help us to spot bad fruit quickly and then run to the Father for directions. Hopefully over time such behavior will be an automatic red flag telling us this is someone who may think they belong to Jesus, but who really needs to know Jesus. If they are approachable, don't run. Stay and talk to them, pray for them, help them get on the right path.

CHAPTER ELEVEN

JESUS ISN'T ABOUT LOVE

Combative Encounters

It shouldn't come as a surprise that encounters between Christians and Moonies can quickly turn combative. Some of these combative encounters could be as simple as someone throwing their arms up and running off. In a different case, a lady angrily announced she would never give anything to a Moonie, but reading my name tag, which clearly said "Unification Church," said she would give to a Lutheran. I took the money without saying a word. But, in many cases the confrontation turned into verbal combat. Because Moonies are often goal oriented, they will often decline to engage and move on. I wasn't always that single minded.

I remember one encounter with a Jehovah's Witness while fundraising door to door. She wanted to argue from the Bible and ran to get an enormous Bible which was awkward to hold and thumb through at the same time. When I pulled out my worn pocket Gideon's New Testament, some of the pages fell out, which I quickly gathered. Finding my quote, I handed the small Bible to her. She was apparently intimidated by the worn condition of my Bible and was now amazed, asking, "You would hand me your weapon?" The idea seemed silly to me, although I didn't let her know that. The Bible is what it is. The only one who should feel strange about a Bible, or who would see the Bible as a weapon poised against them, is one who fundamentally disagrees with the Bible itself. Certainly, the devil doesn't like a well read Bible. The rest of us argue from the Bible in an effort to understand it. That includes Moonies, who clearly do not follow everything written in the Bible.

Definitely, the picture of a Moonie and a Jehovah's Witness arguing over the meaning of scripture is an extreme example of the foolishness of most of these arguments. Our argument could produce nothing useful. We both argued from an understanding more tangled than last years Christmas lights. At the bottom of the arguing is an approach to each other that is a state of warfare. No one gets terribly hurt, outside of an occasional bruised ego, and in most cases, it seems that both combatants walk away just as assured as ever that they are right and the other person is wrong. Occasionally, we might cause each other to rethink things.

This was the case on one hot afternoon in a mall parking lot where I encountered a man who said he was a pastor. We got into a heated argument over the Bible which was going nowhere. Finally, I'd had enough. Hoping to wrap up on a pleasant note, I said, "At least we can agree that Jesus is about love." The pastor spewed back, "Jesus isn't about love!" Then he stopped himself, horrified at what he had just said. He turned and ran over to his car, got in, and drove away.

He had reframed me as the enemy and let his emotions drive the bus. I knew immediately what he was trying to say: the statement "Jesus is love" draws an incomplete picture. As a Moonie, I was not trained to view this pastor as the enemy, but as a potential ally, even a possible convert. I just wanted some common ground. Unfortunately, this man's attitude towards me drove him to foolishness. As a result, I, a Moonie with rather unbiblical theology, apparently won the argument. Bonhoeffer suggests that we need to reframe our thinking. He points out that the Bible definitely places all things in the hands of Christ Jesus, and that includes all those who are desperately wrong (Bonhoeffer 1955). This pastor was not listening to me long enough to see where my theology was seriously off the rails. I suspect that his immediate switch to an argumentative mode meant he knew of the Unification Church as a "cult," an undesirable. Because he didn't really know anything about who or what the Unification Church was, his scatter-shot attack was entirely ineffective.

The Cults

After the seminary, I was sent to England with our entire class of graduates. I spent several months in London. At one point, I was evangelizing on the street when I was approached by a man who immediately, upon discovering that I was a Moonie, suggested that I was a horrid person, the enemy, etc. I rebuked him. I let him know that if he thought I was wrong, he should be approaching me in Christian love and try to reason with me. This was my first meeting with my friend Ed from the chapter on prayer. Ed apologized and invited me to come with him to church, which is where he was heading.

We were nearly in front of the church, as it turned out. I agreed and went into the church with him. We sat in the balcony. It was a very large church. I don't remember any music; we may have arrived late. The pastor went into a tirade against cults, much to Ed's chagrin. Since I was well aware of the sorts of things being said about the Unification Church, I was not surprised. It gave us something to discuss. How do we disagree in a Christlike manner? How do we approach someone we believe to be flat out wrong?

As it was, Ed and I became friends. I wasn't converting him, and he wasn't converting me, though he wanted to. Ed was a typical Christian, committed to the basics of the faith, and that was it. Ed had done his best to emulate his pastor's message. It would have been wonderful if the pastor would have encouraged his congregation to pray.

In the same way, the pastor who shouted "Jesus isn't about love" in the earlier parking lot incident could have said, "Let's pray for wisdom," instead of allowing himself to spiral out into foolishness.

All too often, the picture of Christians in this world is the person sitting back and wagging their finger at everything they see as wrong. Christians forget that we have access to real power through prayer. I believe that prayer has power, even if it's the prayer of a voodoo witch doctor. But, prayer rooted in faith in God and in Jesus Christ, naming the name of Jesus and backed up by the Holy Spirit, has power above and beyond every other power on this earth. Christians falter because they spend far more time complaining and criticizing and not nearly enough time praying, especially praying together.

The Band

While I was in England, the English Unification Church decided to put on an evangelizing tour of the country. At one stop, somewhere up north, possibly Leeds or Manchester, I don't really remember, we were booked into a civic hall with two auditoriums. As we were setting up for the event, a group of Christians gathered outside with anti-Moon banners. We were traveling with a brass band, so we all went outside with the brass band to lighten the mood.

As it happened, the Glenn Miller Orchestra was booked into the other hall. As our brass band gathered out front and let loose, the Glenn Miller tour bus pulled up. When the musicians on the bus saw another brass band, they came piling off the bus, grabbing their instruments, and joined in. Within minutes, the plaza in front of the auditorium was packed with happy brass playing up a storm.

Needless to say, the protesters were overwhelmed and slipped away long before the impromptu jam session was finished. Most people are repelled by angry protest, but are drawn to joyful celebration. It really doesn't matter if the protesters are right or wrong. Even if we don't agree with the basic message, it is hard to walk away from a happy sound. As Joni Mitchell says, "Happiness is the best face lift."

One tiny American church who gets far too much publicity is Westboro Baptist Church. Their public demonstrations against homosexuality, against Catholics and Jews, and even against the American military would seem to be chasing people away from Christ in large numbers, while drawing almost no one to Christ.

Not all things are peaches and cream, even in the Bible. There is a definite harsh side to the Biblical account. There are things that make God angry. God's anger is first mentioned in Genesis and carries through to the end of the Book of Revelation. Unfortunately, that message uncoupled from the hope, the healing and the deliverance of the gospel creates a repulsive picture.

I get together weekly with a number of men where we gather to make music and share communion. We honor Jesus and the Holy Spirit, but several of them will not go to church, any church. Something in the Christianity of their youth has left them with a distaste for the church, either because of their moral failings or, in far too many cases, because of the failings of the church. And yet, most of them love Jesus. The few that don't are still willing to join with us while we praise his name.

Loving Jesus, but not the body of Christ, is a paradox, and there is the conundrum. Is the experience these men have had of the body of Christ, the Church, not an accurate representation of Jesus? Or, is the Jesus the Church is compared to not the real Jesus? My answer would be both. The disciple who leaned on Jesus' breast (John 13:25) in the most familiar way, who then sees him in a vision decades later, "fell at His feet as dead" (Revelations 1:17). Everyone I know who has had deep encounters in the spirit has said that the experience is both wonderful and frightening. As one says jokingly, if you meet a real angel, you will wish you were wearing adult diapers.

The Body of Christ

Those of us who love the body of Christ, the Church, as I do, can point to many things that don't represent Christ well. It is tempting to point out other denominations, other church cultures, or well-known evangelists who fail to represent Christ well, but the truth is that there are probably good examples of un-Christlike behavior happening in your own church body. We are called to have grace and to try to steer the immature in better directions. Did I mention, with grace?

Back to the weekly men's meeting. Our group loves to play music, worship music sometimes, but mostly secular music. We do stay away from music that celebrates the vulgar or sinful. We allow drinking, as did Jesus. We have removed members for drunkenness or excessive vulgarity. And, we always celebrate with communion. The group does include pastors, deacons and worship staff, and we love to pray for each other. But, as I said, there are several there for whom that is their only experience of church. These are those I would have to call orphans from the body of Christ. I have seen several growing in their relationship with the Lord. It is a place where Catholics and Protestants talk candidly with each other. It should not be a substitute for the church, but the sort of place where the various parts of the body of Christ connect in a deeper way. What makes this gathering work is the ability of the group to put aside theological and denominational differences, to consciously overlook inadequacies in Christian practice, while we all just as consciously draw closer to Jesus in so many quiet ways. I am sure that many don't know they are being drawn to Jesus.

It would be appropriate to interject a recent event pertaining to this group. There was a gentleman who had attended our weekly meeting on and off for more than a year. He was not a musician, so he tended to remain in the background, usually staying quiet. However, because he had a drip bag feeding antibiotics to a badly infected knee that refused to heal, we took time on several occasions to pray for him. We were aware that he did not attend church. As it turned out, he was hospitalized for a different issue. We didn't know him well and only found out about it by accident. But, we decided to cancel our Tuesday meeting and take a group to his hospital room to play music and pray for him. To say that this man was delighted would be a gross understatement. Moreover, one of our group, who was also not a musician, but was a former pastor, took a great deal of time talking with him while the rest of us played music. The pastor discovered that our hospitalized friend really did have a love for Jesus, but he had spent so much time in church as a youth that he really didn't want to go back. We were able to reconnect our friend to Jesus and to help him find joy again. He went on to be with the Lord less than a week later. Castigating this man for poor Christian practice would have served no good purpose; loving him back to Jesus was worth every second of our time.

Letting Your Hair Down

As I mentioned, I spent two years studying for a Masters of Religious Education at Unification Theological Seminary. Besides having published theologians from several denominations on staff as professors, the seminary also invited well known theologians to speak. I myself organized something which we called The Global Congress of World Religions, which brought together Christian and non-Christian religious leaders for face to face discussions.

I noticed that during conferences the theologians tended to be somewhat guarded. In the evenings, many of them would retire to a local pub to discuss further. The Moonies didn't drink alcohol, but several of us would follow and sip soda. At the pub, the discussions would become much livelier and more candid. In the pub, the rules all change. It is not permissible to quote a pub statement in an academic discussion, so it is much easier for the academics to be free to think out loud without repercussion. Beer helps.

I noticed the same guarded behavior during a conference on African religions which I helped to host. Most of the invited participants were African, and on the first day the participants arrived dressed in Western suits, typical for academics. Our faculty adviser, who was white, arrived wearing a full-length African dashiki. On the next day, all of the Africans wore dashikis. The conference papers and the discussions were all taped and transcribed, except for the last day of the conference. There was nothing surprising that came out during these discussions, that is, until the last day, which was an open discussion and not recorded. Off mic, the discussion suddenly became a fascinating mix of stories that clearly mixed ancient tribal beliefs with Christian religious beliefs. Hindsight being 20-20, I would love to reframe all of the conference topics to bring that out in the recorded conference.

Ultimately, the problem is one of posturing. I know that one of the professors at Unification Theological Seminary became too closely involved with the Unification Church and lost his position at another seminary, where he had taught for many years. He had become an advocate for the Unification Church, which did not sit well with his colleagues at the other school. Our actions and our statements are all being sifted.

Another one of my professors was being challenged by his own church, where he was and had been a pastor for 25 years. His ordination was being challenged by his denomination as well. The charge against him: he was teaching at a non-Christian seminary. His defense: he was teaching the same thing as he would at any seminary. He refused to back down.

In the course of the battle with his denomination, a set of our term papers disappeared, we assumed to the board judging the matter of his ordination. My own paper was on Paul's efforts to bring together the Greek and Hebrew churches. The topic would be just as valid in a Baptist or a Presbyterian or even a Catholic seminary. The professor did keep his ordination, but was removed as pastor of the church he had served for so many years. We, as Christians, are an unfortunately contentious lot.

Just the other day, I overheard two gentlemen talking at the gym. One assured the other that they had successfully booted their pastor out. He seemed quite pleased with himself. Unfortunately, I know of several such attempts in my local area. One forced the pastor out, and another caused the pastor to give up and resign. In still another case, the board voted out the pastor, only to have the congregation vote the board out and retain the pastor.

Clearly, public representatives of the church, be they pastors or teachers, as well as academics, have good reason to be wary of their public positions or statements. There are good reasons to review the representatives of our faith, but any such review requires great care and grace. "But if you bite and devour one another, take heed that you are not consumed by one another" (Galatians 5:15). It seems that often Christians are their own worst enemy. A lack of grace towards those censured is a sign of a definitely un-Christian attitude: "Do not rejoice when your enemy falls, and let not your heart be glad when he stumbles, lest the LORD see it and be displeased, and turn away his anger from him" (Proverbs 24:17-18).

Right, Wrong and Christ

All too often as people, Christian and non-Christian alike, our instinct is to judge a situation and then want to speak out our agreement or disagreement. For Bonhoeffer, this is eating from the Tree of the Knowledge of Good and Evil. When this is done in the name of Christ, the result is a Christian Pharisee as covered previously.

The Pharisee is not necessarily a hypocrite in the sense of preaching right and wrong, but secretly violating those principles. The Pharisee may be leading an exemplary life by the legal standards of the Bible. The Pharisee may have perfect Biblical doctrine. But, by failing to come into close relationship with the living Jesus so that the breath of God, the Holy Spirit, removes the judgment and replaces it with a desire to connect all things to Christ, the Pharisee repulses the world, creating the spiritual world of the clearly saved performing religious activities and assigning all other activities to the secular world. But for Bonhoeffer, there is no distinction between sacred and secular because everything belongs to Christ (Bonhoeffer 1955, 203-204). The world just hasn't figured out yet who is in charge. All Christians are priests in his kingdom (Revelations 1:5-6).

Does this mean that the law of God is no longer valid, or that the fear of God has ceased to be? Bonhoeffer is clear that this is not the case. The law is still valid, but the Pharisee has become an unauthorized advocate for God, decoupling the law and the gospel by interjecting himself between the law and the gospel. Jesus did not come to recruit lawyers for heaven. God sent Jesus to reconnect us to Himself. When we are reconnected, we will do the will of heaven and will have the right words to say. For Bonhoeffer, this reconnected person is a new being (see also: Tillich 1955) who has become responsive to God by hearing from God and putting into immediate action the desire of heaven. In this, obedience is freedom:

> Obedience knows what is good and does it, and freedom dares to act, and abandons to God the judgment of good and evil... The responsible man delivers up himself and his deed to God (Bonhoeffer 1955, 248-249).

God had a hold of me all through the years in which I called myself an atheist, a Buddhist, and a Moonie. He was slowly reshaping me until the day I could come close and hear His voice more clearly. I had all the intellectual guns to shoot down any finger wagging Christian Pharisee, and I successfully did so on more than one occasion. But, the closer I got to God, the more difficult it became to resist a godly person. More importantly, I could not resist the "still small voice" (I Kings 19:12).

The Christian Pharisee steps back from the world, creating the false separation between God's space (His Kingdom, the sacred, the spiritual) and the world. The danger here is that this creates an us and them scenario. The Pharisee sees themselves as God's elect. "A Christianity which withdraws from the world falls victim to the unnatural and the irrational, to presumption and self-will" (Bonhoeffer 1955, 197). Without knowing it, God's elect fall victim to what Jonathan Edwards calls "undiscerned spiritual pride":

> One cause of errors attending a great Revival of Religion, is undiscerned Spiritual Pride. The first and worst cause of errors, that prevail in such a state of things is spiritual pride. This is the main door by which the devil comes into the hearts of those who are zealous for the advancement of religion. It is the chief inlet of smoke from the bottomless pit, to darken the mind and mislead the judgment. This is the main handle by which the devil has hold of religious persons, and the chief source of all the mischief that he introduces, to clog and hinder a work of God... This cause of error is the main spring, or at least the main support, of all the rest. Till this disease is cured, medicines are in vain applied to heal other diseases. It is by this that the mind defends itself in other errors, and guards itself against light, by

which it might be corrected and reclaimed. The spiritually proud man is full of light already, he does not need instruction, and is ready to despise the offer of it. But if this disease be healed, other things are easily rectified (Edwards 1829, 338-339).

Edwards is someone who moves easily between the glories of the grace of God to a withering declamation of the horrors of a life of sin. Edwards fully understood the importance of God's law and the importance of the gospel of grace. There is no way to properly balance the two positions outside of the direct and immediate leading of God. It is the inability to hear God in the moment that leads the Church into destructive quarrels within the Church. These quarrels lead the unchurched to be repulsed. And yet, the unchurched are those to whom Jesus Christ is calling. This is a failure to understand that, above all, Jesus is about love, and that all things belong to Him already. The very person whom the Church has written off may be the very person who holds the most promise for God's work. No one would have believed that Saul of Tarsus was called of God, not even after he was converted on the road to Damascus, but Ananias obeyed the call to approach him (Acts 9:10-18), and Barnabas championed him (Acts 9:27). Thank God for their hearing ears and obedience to the call of God.

CHAPTER TWELVE

ARM BANDS

Sunnies

At the time I was a member of the Unification Church, our approach and our belief system was apocalyptic, full of hope for the kingdom of God "on earth as it is in heaven" (Matthew 6:10). Our expectation was to be persecuted, but to prevail.

Some time, long after I had left the church, I was in a discussion with one man who suggested the Moonies he had met all looked tired. My comment was that they probably were tired. The Moonies that are most commonly encountered, and still occasionally are encountered, are fundraisers. Fundraising teams would spend long hours selling candy, flowers, or other trinkets for donations. These teams would start early with an hour of prayer, breakfast and then travel to begin fundraising busy street corners or businesses when they opened. In the evening, we would fundraise in restaurants and bars until well past midnight and travel home exhausted. Home was a crowded apartment or hotel room. Someone still had to count the money, roll coins and so on. These were very long and exhausting days with very few breaks.

I was with one fundraising team when our van was pulled over late at night for weaving on the road. The entire team was asleep except for the driver and myself. We were struggling desperately to stay awake and therefore weaving badly. Since no one had been drinking, the officer warned us and let us go. That was the month that I never got more than three hours of sleep in a night. I remember falling asleep on the toilet more than once. I would wake up with a red ring around my backside. Never-the-less, our disposition was almost always upbeat and cheerful. People just can't help but be drawn by a happy face.

The warmth and the close community are the Moonies' best recruiting tool. Moonies called this "love bombing." This works the best on young people that are without a strong social network. In my case, I had just finished college, did not want to go home, and wasn't sure which direction to take next. My friends had all either packed up and left or were on their way soon. I had a pull towards religion, but didn't like any of the alternatives in front of me. I had come home from working at my summer job laying irrigation lines when a bright and happy Italian girl knocked on my door. She invited me to a meeting that evening, and I immediately accepted without knowing much about it. Before long I was at a weekend retreat where the feeling of community was strong. I became a Moonie a week later.

Let's be real. Happiness sells. Sun Myung Moon once said, "We shouldn't be called Moonies, we should be called Sunnies!"

On the day of the Yankee Stadium rally June 1, 1976, the Moonies had arrived early in large numbers, myself included. In late afternoon before the rally a heavy rainstorm came sweeping into the stadium. A wall of water came rolling across the partial roof above where I was sitting. Wind and pounding rain filled the stadium. The Moonies having the attitude that this was an attack of the devil all came forward to stand in the rain. We began to sing "You Are My Sunshine" simultaneously without prompting. In a matter of minutes, the rain passed on as fast as it had arrived. The sun came out again and the stadium was dried out and put back in order before the rally began that evening. The Moonies handled all opposition, whether natural or spiritual, with an aggressive cheerfulness.

Confronting Police

At the time, the newspapers and magazines had numerous articles telling lurid tales of happenings going on in the Unification Church. We were quickly labeled a cult. This meant that the police would try to stop us from fundraising, which led to occasional confrontations with the law.

In one small town, I had been stopped from fund raising, so I asked directions to the town offices, intending to examine the ordinances that prohibited fundraising door-to-door. The church by this time had become sophisticated enough to challenge some of these laws in court, usually with success. After some hemming and hawing by the clerk and a discussion in the offices behind the desk, I was informed that the ordinance was verbal, not written.

Generally, a Moonie fundraiser is in a team of six to ten fundraisers that travel by van. The fundraiser is dropped off in the morning, sometimes alone, sometimes in groups of two to four. In the case above, I was alone and wouldn't be picked up until dinner time. This leads to a difficulty when you are stopped. This was the days in which affordable cell phones did not exist. In a very small town, it is best to comply and sit and wait.

In a larger town, the situation is different. In one locality there were four of us fundraising a remote, but busy, four-way intersection. The police stopped us. We stopped and waited for about fifteen minutes after they left before we started again. An hour later, the same police returned. They were now a bit miffed at us. We stopped again and waited twenty minutes before starting again. An hour or two later, the same police returned. They were now visibly upset with us, so we assured them that we would stop.

There we were, four people bent on saving the world by our own sweat and blood, but having to sit on our behinds for another five hours. It wasn't long before one of the girls couldn't stand it any longer and begged to be allowed to fundraise. I was the senior member of the crew and reluctantly said yes. Not surprisingly, the police appeared again. They were very angry and were intent on taking the girl into custody. I assured them that it was my fault, that I was in charge, and that they should take me instead. The officer grabbed me and thrust me into the back seat. He was kicking me in the behind as I went head first through the rear door of the cruiser. The other officer was in the driver's seat and seemed calm. There was a minor problem. The angry officer's night stick had been thrown over the seat so that it was lying diagonal from the back seat to the back of the front seat. I had to move it. I reached out and took hold of it. Remember that the officer behind me was kicking me. As I lifted the stick, I looked up at the driver. His eyes were as big as saucers. He was clearly imagining that night stick clouting him in the side of the head. I calmly handed the stick to him and got in.

The angry officer slammed the door behind me and got in the passenger seat, slamming his door. He had no idea what had just happened. The officer at the wheel began to drive slowly through a parking lot. He clearly had no heart to take me into custody. After driving about twenty feet, he convinced his angry partner that I had gotten the message and they should release me. Why? I stayed calm and courteous, even pleasant, in a tense situation.

On another occasion, I was fundraising at a traffic light on one end of a freeway overpass in Chicago. I had bags of peanuts. I am not sure how, but officers on the freeway below spotted me and pulled into the median of the freeway below. Using the loudspeaker in the police cruiser, they told me to stop. As always, I immediately stopped. Since I didn't have a vehicle, I couldn't leave. As usual, I was waiting for them to leave so that I could start again. These officers were having none of it. They made a U-turn in the middle of the freeway and came up the exit ramp. I was immediately handcuffed. I had a large box filled with bags of peanuts which I was ordered to place in the trunk of the police cruiser. With my cuffed hands behind my back, I looked at the officer. He quickly realized I had no way to do what he had asked.

He uncuffed me so that I could put the peanuts into the trunk and then he recuffed me.

The ride back to the station was interesting. I learned that the reason the officers were upset was that a colleague had been suspended from the force after beating up a Hare Krishna fundraiser. Hare Krishna is a well-known fundamentalist Hindu cult. Having met Krishna fundraisers in parking lots from time to time, I wasn't surprised that the officer had had issues with one of them. The Krishna fundraisers that I had encountered tended to be defiant and combative. I was sympathetic with the officers' friend even if I couldn't condone his actions.

In one case, I met some Hare Krishnas who were disguised as Moonies, complete with wigs (they usually have shaved heads), white shirts and ties. In only one case was I aware of Moonies being combative. This was a Japanese team whose over insistence on money made following behind them, several days later, a long day of apologizing with very little to show for it.

In the squad car, the two officers and I began to discuss religion. As it happened, one of the officers was taking seminary classes on the side. I told him that I had recently graduated from the Moonie's seminary. We got back to the station, and one officer began to write the report while we continued to discuss religion and seminary and beliefs. When the report writer asked the other officer what the charge should be, they decided to release me instead. We parted on friendly terms. Again, I had remained calm and courteous, even sympathetic. The result was a fruitful discussion, even if the fundraising was truncated. No one was converted either way, but we were able to part on friendly terms.

One of my friends from the seminary was captaining a fundraising team when he was arrested while trying to wire a large amount of loose cash to a bank account in another state. He hadn't shaved and was looking a bit seedy. Add it all together, and he suddenly became a suspect in a bank robbery in a neighboring state. He spent several days in jail before they realized their mistake and released him. He thought it comical and spent his time in jail trying to recruit for the Moonies.

Stay calm, don't panic, and always try to be pleasant even if things aren't going your way. Moonies expect that things won't always go their way, so it was easier to stay courteous, even genuinely pleasant in difficult circumstances.

Confronting the Press

Shortly after my graduation from the seminary, I was sent to Wisconsin to be the "state leader." This amounted to running one center in Milwaukee and keeping tabs on two couples, one far off in Green Bay. When I arrived, the previous leader met me at the door, said congratulations, and promptly left. I was on my own. I quickly discovered that the center was deeply in debt, owing to a large evangelizing campaign that had come through Milwaukee, leaving a large stack of unpaid bills. Having unpaid bills is not a good way to operate, especially for an evangelical church. It is hard to hold yourself out as a moral authority while leaving vendors unpaid. It was clear that my first job would have to be paying down the debt.

While I was practiced at selling candy and flowers on street corners, I really hated it. Polling the members at the Milwaukee center, it was clear that I was not alone. One of the members worked with some friends doing small remodeling jobs. As it happened, I had done stage carpentry in college. I knew how to swing a hammer and draw up blueprints. So, we launched a remodeling business. By the end of the year, we had cleared most of the debt away.

We would hold church services in the living room on Sundays. We even got some of the neighbors to attend. (The next-door neighbor was American Indian. She taught me how to make pan bread). Like all Moonie centers, there was extensive daily prayer and plenty of time for Bible study as well as studying the Moonie text *Divine Principle*.

I had one member assigned to witness, but she wasn't happy with it and wasn't being terribly productive. She had no support to speak of, so it was a surprise when we got a call from someone who wanted to attend a lecture on the *Divine Principle*. When the young lady showed up, I suspected she was from the press. When she arrived, she was ready with a notebook and pen. I gave her the usual introductory lecture and answered her questions. I was not a bit surprised, afterwards, when she admitted to being from a local television station. She asked if she could bring a cameraman and interview me. It became clear she wanted to do a secrets of the Moonie cult sort of expose. I declined the interview. She said, "What if we tape you in shadow and disguise your voice?" That would clearly make it appear that something clandestine was going on. Begrudgingly, I said yes to an interview, but no shadows or weird stuff.

A few days later, the young reporter came back with her cameraman to interview me. As it turned out, the burning question had to do with a local restaurant that was run by a couple who were church members. The press wanted to know if this was in fact a Moonie restaurant. I answered truthfully that it was not owned or operated by the church, evading what she truly wanted to know. When I walk into a restaurant, if there is a fat Buddha in the lobby with offerings in front of him, I assume the owners are Buddhist. Or, if I go into a Mexican restaurant with pictures of the Virgin of Guadalupe on the wall, I assume the owner is Catholic. But in most restaurants, there is no way to know what the religions of the owner, or the wait staff, or cooks are. It is not usually pertinent. I said as much. I went on to suggest that the very question implied that there was something wrong with Moonies operating a restaurant or other business. I told the reporter we did operate a business out of the center as a sole proprietor partnership, therefore not owned by the church. We did not make any effort to disclose our religious affiliation, not that we were hiding it. Finally, I asked the reporter if she thought we should be wearing armbands to let people know we were Moonies. There are plenty of Jews in Milwaukee, so I am sure the allusion struck home.

The press is very good at stirring up muck without thinking the question all the way through to the end. It shouldn't be a surprise that the reporter's in-depth report never made it to the evening news. As always, I took a measured response. As in so many situations, the question posed was antagonistic, but I answered slowly and calmly. I then took her question to the logical conclusion. I suppose that if I had answered with an animated counter attack, the reporter could have found a way to edit the response so that my answer appeared to be evasive, leaving out anything that challenged the question itself.

I was on the security detail for the New Yorker Hotel for a short time. The New Yorker was an aging hotel that was a prominent NYC landmark. It sits directly across from Penn Station. At the time, it was owned by the Unification Church and had a large number of members living there. The press camped out in buildings across the street. I remember seeing a picture in the newspaper of a Moonie shaving taken from across the street through his bathroom window. It seemed a little creepy and invasive.

Late one Sunday morning, when most of the residents were piling onto buses or vans to travel to Moon's residence north of the city for a Sunday morning talk, a staff member rushed up to me saying there was something wrong with the freight elevator. I followed him and was standing there while he forced the door open. There before me was the body of a young man lying in a pool of blood and brains. Most of his head was gone. He had fallen down the shaft, crashing through the roof of the elevator car.

I quickly alerted the head of security and we cordoned off the area. A call was put in to the police station which was less than a block away. Press trucks were at the front door before the police could get there.

The cause of death was not clear. The freight elevator was very old and didn't have a call function. It was difficult to know where it was. The staff was known to force the safety doors open to look up and down the shaft to see where the elevator car was. This young man may have slipped and fallen down the shaft. His diary found in his room indicated a severely depressed young man. Moonie cheerful love bombing and busy work ethic didn't work for everyone. It was quickly postulated that the young man may have committed suicide, at least that was the spin the press put on it. One newspaper managed to get photographs of certain pages of his diary which they published to great fanfare.

It was an unfortunate incident made worse by the ghoulish interest of the press and ultimately the public. As Moonies we became used to feeling that we were under a microscope. We were aggressive but careful with our behavior in public because of it.

The Government and Moon

Sun Myung Moon had favor with several prominent conservatives, including Ronald Reagan, owing to his efforts to counteract Communism in Japan, Korea and elsewhere. The Reagan administration used Moonie contacts to funnel illegal funds to the Contra fighters in Nicaragua. Top Moonies were called to testify before congress during the Iran-Contra investigation.

As the Unification Church campaigns grew larger, the opposition became more intense, it was inevitable that the favor Moon enjoyed would sour. Several states and municipalities attempted to enact laws to stop Moonie fundraisers. The Moonies were quick to lawyer up. Attempts to stop Moonie fundraisers were defeated in the courts.

The IRS became involved. Tax auditors were sent into the national headquarters of the Unification Church. They set up offices there and spent seven years auditing the books. They eventually found what they were looking for. Money had been brought from Korea and deposited into a church account and then later moved to Moon's personal accounts, but never reported as income. As a result, taxes that should have been paid were not paid. Moon was charged in Federal court. I believe the government assumed he would flee the country. Moon had no intention of leaving.

In 1982, Moon was sentenced to 18 months in Federal prison, of which he served 13 before being released. The state department then attempted to have him deported, but the case was dismissed as double jeopardy. Having been tried and sentenced, and having served his time, it was unfair to try him again for the same crime. All of this, the Moonies took in stride, assuming it to be nothing more than Satan trying to stop the Kingdom of Heaven.

Offensive Christianity

A few years back, the company I was working for had taken on a contract to do some of the work on a new Planned Parenthood office building and clinic here in Houston. The owners of the company that employed me are genuinely nice people, but not Christian. Protesters lined up across the street yelling and waving signs picturing aborted fetuses. I don't agree with abortion, however I am quite sure that nothing positive occurred that day. The company simply took down their logo so there was nothing to show on the news but a brick office building. My pastor was intending to take me to lunch that day, but I informed him that it was probably not a good day to show up. The angry protesters certainly didn't win any new hearts and minds to their cause.

Stink bombs, snipers and protesters chained to the door don't leave an attractive image. What if, instead, women with babies sit in front of the clinic? Is there anything that will bring a young girl thinking of aborting her baby to her knees faster than a little baby? Near our church is a women's shelter set up to help unwed mothers. They have found that the best answer they have is a sonogram machine. Once that young girl sees the developing baby in her womb, it is hard not to choose life for that child.

On another issue: most Bible believing Christians have a hard time with accepting homosexuality as normal. However, Westboro Baptist Church, with its slogan implying that God hates homosexuals using a vulgar slur, does not help. This is especially true when the Church as a whole has come late to the issue and is struggling to adequately respond. Several large, biblically liberal denominations have already capitulated.

Christians will not maintain the moral high ground unless we think these issues through, slowly and deliberately, and give good clear answers which agree with the Bible. It would be better to answer before the press has already had a field day with the issue. By now, the courts and academic institutions have lined up against any sort of sexual normality. Any attempt by Christians to argue for a healthy human sexuality is already starting on its back foot. I do believe this is an important topic for the church to tackle, but only by careful and deliberate response.

My brother and I went to a recent exhibit of an Italian artist at a local museum. This particular artist definitely disliked the church. Some of his pieces were down right childish. I am thinking of disembodied hands hanging from the ceiling "flipping the bird," or a horse (it appeared to have been an actual stuffed horse) lying dead with a spear thrust through it bearing a sign with the letters INRI ("Iesus Nazarenus Rex Iudaeorum," Latin for "Jesus of Nazareth, the King of the Jews"), the same sign that Pilate had nailed above the crucified Christ (John 19:19). My brother and I began commenting back and forth, "This man has a problem with the church." Other than technical proficiency, there was nothing terribly compelling about his work, unless the viewer also dislikes

Christianity and delights in the childish rant. For the church to respond in kind would be a horrible mistake.

On the other hand, there is contemporary artist Makoto Fujimura, who calls for culturally positive art, what he refers to as "Culture Care." He has been appointed Director of the *Brehm Center for Worship, Theology, and the Arts* at Fuller Theological Seminary. In addition, He has founded the International Arts Movement:

> We value an approach to life and work that is rehumanizing, generative, enterprising, and generous that fosters an environment for wrestling with the deep questions of art, faith and humanity (IAM value statement from the website: www. iamculturecare.com, accessed 3/9/2019).

The whole thrust of his artistic outlook is different from the various movements that champion the art of rebellion and disdain. It shows in his art. Fujimura's paintings are works that exude peace and tranquility. I would love to have one on my wall hovering over my morning quiet times with the Lord. Fujimura has successful showings before fine arts gatherings where he comfortably talks about the Christian principles that infuse his art.

A Christian should have an entirely different approach to the world. That approach should be compelling, and it should ultimately bring peace.

> I have said these things to you, that in me you may have peace. In the world you will have tribulation. But take heart; I have overcome the world (John 16:33).

There are times when the Christian is called to stand in opposition, but with grace and humility. This was the case for

Dietrich Bonhoeffer and many other Christian leaders under Adolf Hitler, to say nothing of other Christians throughout church history. As Hitler and the Nazi party came to power, Bonhoeffer was compelled to publicly oppose the Nazis. When the Jewish children were thrown out of schools, Bonhoeffer opened schools for them. He was silenced by the Nazis. He was jailed and eventually hung for his opposition. Bonhoeffer is by no means an isolated case. There are many times when a Christian is called to oppose, and this includes the above-mentioned debates. Christian opposition must necessarily stay in keeping with Christian character: prayerful, humble, reasonable and firm. The rule remains: the law and the gospel work together, never apart (Bonhoeffer 1955, 197).

CHAPTER THIRTEEN

HERE BELOW

Not Gnostic

Many of the new religious movements which Christians refer to as cults, if not most, are to one degree or another Gnostic. This is particularly true of those groups with Hindu roots, such as Hare Krishna or Transcendental Meditation. Similarly, Buddhists, Sikhs and of course openly Gnostic groups like the Rosicrucians all share a disdain for the material life and seek a transcendent spiritual life.

The Gnostic Christians were some of the first heretics that the early church fathers had to deal with. It seems that transcending this flesh has been a quest of the religious since the beginning of time. It is still very popular with Christians who would never call themselves Gnostic. Jesus promised a newness in the flesh:

> The one who conquers, I will make him a pillar in the temple of my God. Never shall he go out of it, and I will write on him the name of my God, and the name of the city of my God, the new Jerusalem, which comes down from my God out of heaven, and my own new name (Revelations 3:12).

Notice that the new Jerusalem comes down to earth. The one who conquers is here on earth. When Jesus teaches his disciples the fundamentals of prayer, he says, "Pray... Your kingdom come, your will be done, on earth as it is in heaven" (Matthew 6:9-10).

The early church was adamant, the Gnostic dismissal of the world of physical matter was missing the point. God made a good world, and in fact the apostle Paul is very clear about this:

> For what can be known about God is plain to them, because God has shown it to them. For his invisible attributes, namely, his eternal power and divine nature, have been clearly perceived, ever since the creation of the world, in the things that have been made. So they are without excuse (Romans 1:19-20).

God is plainly seen in the beauty of the material world. Paul continues on to enumerate all the problems that happen when humankind fails to recognize and acknowledge that beauty. The flesh that Paul so often refers to in a negative connotation is not material flesh, but the twisted thought life, the lusts and ambitions, the pride of men and women striving to build a world without falling on their face before God.

The Moonies, on the other hand, have a viewpoint opposite to that of the Gnostics; they are trying to build the kingdom of heaven here on earth. Their vision of spirituality has more to do with using the things of the spirit to pursue an earthly agenda.

Boots on the Ground

I never once heard a discussion of salvation by faith from a Moonie. The emphasis was always on actions. New recruits were almost always sent to fundraise and witness. This was, as mentioned, difficult for me personally.

Even though I graduated college with a Bachelor of Fine Arts in Theater, I was a designer and technician, not an actor. All drama majors must act, regardless of their emphasis. The one major role that I played in college was a frightened young man in Pinter's "The Birthday Party." To this day, I maintain it was a case of type casting. I was never comfortable performing before strangers.

The Unification Church took me to the very place I liked the least. On my first day out street witnessing, I was paired with a young Frenchman who would push me into the greeting and then maintain he couldn't speak English, forcing me to do the talking. His English was just fine. In fact, I thought his accent lent a certain air of charm.

It wasn't hard for me to recognize that I had to become more outgoing. In fact, I had taken speech classes in college for that very reason. Acting was required of all drama majors, even scene designers. Like the speech classes, I viewed acting as good training, or good therapy. I never learned to enjoy street witnessing or fundraising. In fact, it would be accurate to say I hated it. However, I always felt it was good to keep trying to do it better. I never successfully won a convert to Moon's church. Hindsight being twenty-twenty, that is one less thing I have to regret.

The church engaged in large evangelical campaigns involving hundreds of street witnessers handing out tickets and flyers, and cold calling people in coordination with large scale ad campaigns. I was personally involved in three very large campaigns: Moon's Madison Square Garden rally in 1974, his Yankee Stadium rally in 1976 and a rally on the national mall in Washington DC, also in 1976.

Kingdom Building

The Unification Church was always busy buying prominent properties. The attitude was always clear: buy highly visible or noteworthy properties and never sell. Once the church owned a property, the rule was that it now belonged to the Kingdom of Heaven and could never be sold. The most significant property the church purchased was the Hotel New Yorker. Diagonally across the street from Penn Station, the forty-two-story hotel was a notable landmark, visible from New Jersey. I lived there for two years until the time of my exit from the church at the very end of 1981.

The church was also involved in academia, sponsoring large, well-funded conferences such as the International Conference on the Unity of the Sciences (ICUS) and The Congress of World Religions, which I organized. ICUS excelled at bringing prominent scientists, philosophers and religious leaders from all over the world to discuss scientific and moral issues. Moon's own address to the fourth conference in 1975 is entitled "The Centrality of Science and Absolute Values," and mirrors the general tenor of the conferences. Participants included a long list of Nobel laureates. In addition, the church sponsored other forums for academic discussion such as the Professors World Peace Academy (PWPA). After my time in the church, PWPA gained control of the University of Bridgeport by bailing out the heavily in debt school. The partnership was acrimonious and the school was able to eliminate Moonie involvement after regaining financial stability. The church's programs have changed names and form considerably over time, but the church has stayed active in the academic world.

Jonathan Wells, a colleague of mine from Unification Theological Seminary, established an institute at the University of Washington to argue Intelligent Design. He appears in *Expelled: No Intelligence Allowed*, Ben Stein's humorous documentary on scientific and academic resistance to admitting that God really did create the universe and everything in it.

The church had started schools in Korea as well as the seminary in upstate New York. Moon expressed interest in starting a university somewhere near New York City. That never occurred, but the church has opened other schools since my involvement.

In addition to academics, the church was heavily involved in politics. Shortly after joining, I was moved to a side organization called Freedom Leadership Foundation which sought to counter the influence of Communism. The church had connections with several anti-Communist politicians through Moon's campaigns against Communism in Japan, where he met Ronald Reagan. At that time, Reagan was active with the World Anti-Communist League (WACL), as well as with Young Americans for Freedom (YAF). The church worked with both of those organizations and kept several lobbyists on Capitol Hill.

Moon also ventured into the news business with the New York newspaper *News World* in 1976. News World Communications has gone on to own several newspapers and magazines in the US, Japan and Korea.

Moon was also interested in the arts. He created the Little Angels Children's Folk Ballet in Korea. He bought the Manhattan Center directly next to the New Yorker Hotel and attempted to turn it into a television studio. He also purchased the ailing New York City Symphony, which made the Manhattan Center its home.

He had purchased a tool maker in Germany as well as industries in Korea. Many of these entities have changed names and/or have changed their emphasis.

As you can see, Moon and the Unification Church were interested in every area of human endeavor. Moon wanted to change the world to Christian conservative values. He really wanted to create a good world that touched people cradle to grave. He intended the influence to be felt well beyond the confines of the church.

Outside of a few questionable activities of the church, most of these programs are the sorts of things that Christians should be involved in. It seems that we have finally awakened to the fact that this world needs Christians in politics, we need Christians in theater and movie companies, we need Christians in the arts, and we need Christians controlling newspapers and media outlets. While we do have a long tradition of Christian universities and magazines. This misses the point. Having a "Christian" movie is very different from a movie that exudes Christian values, much as Makoto Fujimura's art exudes values that have a Christian source, but without having to have a Christianity label. Fujimura is welcome in Soho galleries where the Christian underpinnings of his art can be freely discussed without becoming overbearing.

There should be no area in which the Unification Church outshines the combined resources of the Christian churches. There are several areas in which the Unification Church failed to excel. This has to do with genuine mercy works such as hospitals, orphanages, drug and alcohol dependence rehabilitation, women's shelters and so on. I am sure the fault is not one of desire, but the church was strategically using its resources where the social impact would be the greatest.

The Spirit World

Not every Moonie battle was aimed at the physical world. For Moonies, the goal was always concrete, but it was not always this-worldly. It was common for Moonies, like Mormons, to pray or fast for those who have already departed. Catholics believe in a purgatory in between heaven and hell and similarly pray for the departed. Some Christians have a more limited view of a place of purification before access to heaven. This justifies prayers for the dead. The Moonies believed that everyone will eventually be restored to unity with God in heaven, a view known as universal reconciliation, universal salvation or simply universalism. For the Moonies, eventual salvation includes Satan. Moon taught that Satan would be the last one saved. By contrast, Biblical Christians adhere to the position that there is no release from hell:

And another angel, a third, followed them, saying with a loud voice, "If anyone worships the beast and its image and receives a mark on his forehead or on his hand, he also will drink the wine of God's wrath, poured full strength into the cup of his anger, and he will be tormented with fire and sulfur in the presence of the holy angels and in the presence of the Lamb. And the smoke of their torment goes up forever and ever, and they have no rest, day or night, these worshipers of the beast and its image, and whoever receives the mark of its name" (Revelations 14:9-11; also: Jude 1:8-13).

the devil who had deceived them was thrown into the lake of fire and sulfur where the beast and the false prophet were, and they will be tormented day and night forever and ever (Revelations 20:10).

Are prayers for the dead, prayers to get them over the hump so to speak, legitimate? I don't really know. My own reading of scripture would say no, but I have friends who adamantly claim otherwise. There is enough ambiguity in scripture to suggest the debate is unnecessary. It won't hurt to pray for the dead. As for praying for the devil or praying for the truly anti-Christ after they are departed, I am pretty sure that scripture is clear, their punishment is eternal. There is no reprieve for Satan.

In any case, the Moonies were believers in prayer and fasting as warfare on the spiritual level. Not only did the Moonies pray for the salvation of ancestors, but they also believed in praying against spiritual enemies attacking individuals, families and nations. There were students in the seminary who had come across deliverance material and were quite excited about it. As a Christian, I have been in deliverance sessions and I am sure that messing with the demonic without the Holy Spirit is a very bad

WM. W. WELLS

idea (Acts 19:13-16). But then, I suppose witches and warlocks do it all the time. To my knowledge, none of these students ever attempted a deliverance session.

I would have to say that 99% of all Moonie prayer and fasting or other acts of "indemnity" were conducted on behalf of the living. Young members would have been unlikely to have known anything about talking to the dead as it wasn't a part of normal Moonie practice.

The Unification Church was devoted first and foremost to changing this world for the better. Moonie moral values were then, and I assume still are, in line with conservative Christian values.

Coram Deo

For Christians, righteousness in the eyes of the world (*coram mundo*) is not enough. Righteousness must be found in the eyes of God (*coram Deo*). Especially for Reformed Christians, this is where the rubber meets the road.

The "Four Spiritual Laws" is a simplification of the above argument: God loves you and has a wonderful plan for your life. We are all born sinful and separated from God. Jesus is the only solution for this sinful condition. Each person must choose for themselves to receive Jesus as their Lord and Savior. In essence, this is an attempt to simplify two thousand years of struggle over what it means to be a Christian into four bullet points.

It is a good place to start. We know God loves us. All we have to do is look at the world He created for us to inhabit (Romans 1:20). Believing that God loves me in particular can be more difficult. The Book of Job is a great example of someone who is struggling with this concept. In fact, most commentaries don't do a very good job of making Job's God look loving.

Sometimes God's love is tender and sweet, but other times it is tough love. When dad shows up with presents, it is easy to feel loved. When dad is giving you a dressing down over something that you have done wrong, it is less easy to feel the love. The God of my Bible is not always happy. Sometimes, it takes years to see the wisdom and the love there. I suppose some of us never see it. Some among us have struggled with experiences that make it difficult to feel loved in any circumstance.

I know many people who grew up in harsh and legalistic churches that find it difficult to accept the fellowship of other Christians. They only knew tough love, but have never been able to feel it as love. I am assuming a benefit of the doubt, that it truly was love. Non-believers are quick to accept sinful behavior. They typically don't really think it is sin. Somewhere in the middle is a place that recognizes sin, but has the merciful reach of God to patiently turn the sinful heart.

The flaw of the Moonies is that they have placed their faith in Sun Myung Moon and his family. It should be abundantly clear that, however wonderful the aspirations of Moon and his followers, they are just as flawed as anyone else. To follow Moon is to follow a blind guide. Jesus says, "Let them alone" (Matthew 15:14).

On one level, Moonies prided themselves in all the negativity of being called a cult. It seemed to reinforce their feeling of being right. Wasn't Jesus persecuted and attacked? Paul's teacher, the Pharisee Gamaliel (Acts 22:3), urged the Jewish council to temper their attacks on the apostles, noting that if they are of God, they will flourish no matter what, and if not, they will gradually disappear (Acts 5:34-39). And so it is, as the media furor and Christian hyperbole has subsided, the Moonies have dwindled. They are still there, but name calling will not make them disappear.

Ultimately, the final question: Is your faith in something or someone here on earth? Is your faith in a son of Adam? Or, is your faith in Jesus Christ, who is sitting at the right hand of God?

CHAPTER FOURTEEN

LIVING IN THE BUBBLE

Choosing Sides

We are people who get excited over all sorts of things. I can get pretty worked up when I am late for an appointment and can't find my car keys. And then there is the excitement of being in a large and focused crowd: a concert, a political rally, a football game, or worship... We are social beings, and group excitement provides positive feedback for our feeling of the rightness of our beliefs, whether it is a belief in our baseball team or a belief in our political party or in our religious beliefs.

In many ways, our ideas of right and wrong, good and bad, or just being on the right team are reinforced every time we talk with someone who agrees with us, or every time we read or hear something that seems to reinforce our personal faith. Christians should join together to build each other up in the faith. "Therefore encourage one another and build one another up, just as you are doing" (I Thessalonians 5:11).

It is for this reason that we attend church, read the Bible, read or listen to other Christian authors, watch videos or television programs of respected Christian teachers and so on. "Do not be led away by diverse and strange teachings, for it is good for the heart to be strengthened by grace" (Hebrews 13:9). We want to hang out with other Christians who are like minded. There is a downside. If we become particularly good at insulating ourselves from the rest of the world, we start to live in a bubble. There is the world inside the bubble, "us," and the world outside, "them." As Cox pointed out in the *Secular City*, the ability to custom tailor our world to suit ourselves is greatly increased in the secular city.

Two recent books tackle the issues of living in a world divided into personal selection groups or tribes: one by self-identified Liberal Democrat Ken Sterns, *Republican Like Me: How I Left the Liberal Bubble and Learned to Love the Right* (Sterns 2017), and the other by the cultural critic Alan Jacobs, *How to Think: A Survival Guide to a World at Odds* (Jacobs 2017).

Jacobs, who teaches at Baylor University, is particularly hard on the academic world because of its self-proclaimed role as the environment of free thinking. He points out that the academic environment enforces boundaries to thinking (Jacobs 2017, 24).

> How often do we say "she really thinks for herself" when someone rejects views that we hold? No: when someone departs from what we believe to be the True Path our tendency is to look for bad influences. She's fallen under the spell of so-and-so. She's been reading to much X or listening to too much Y or watching too much Z. Similarly, people in my line of work always say that we want to promote "critical thinking"—but really, we want our students to think critically only about what they've learned at home and in church, not about what they learn from us (Jacobs 2017, 37).

Jacobs borrows a phrase from Susan Friend Harding, who had begun a study of fundamentalist Christianity and was challenged within the academic community for speaking well of "the repugnant cultural other" (Jacobs 2017, 26). He notes that for the secular academic, the fundamentalist or evangelical Christian is a repugnant cultural other, and the opposite is true as well. For the fundamentalist or evangelical believer, the secular academic is a repugnant cultural other (Jacobs 2017, 27). For Harding, just studying fundamentalism made her feel that she were being asked by her peers, "Are you now, or have you ever been a born-again Christian" (Jacobs 2017, 26)?

As a Moonie, I found myself to be a repugnant cultural other to both the secular academics and the fundamentalist or evangelical Christians. One afternoon, I was street preaching in New York City. A man in a white lab coat stepped in front of me and said, "I have a bed upstairs for you if you would like." I was a little confused until I turned around to realize I was in front of a building that housed a psychiatric facility. I had mistakenly chosen a spot that reinforced every stereotype about the Moonie "cult."

Sterns' book deals specifically with our political divisiveness. His second chapter, "The Party of God," discusses evangelicals and politics. He recalls an interview with evangelical law professor John Inazu:

> He [Inazu] tells of working with a fellow faculty member for several months on a project and afterward having her comment to him with genuine puzzlement, "I don't get you. You are a religious person and yet you care about poor people," a statement made without any recognition that in the United States it is more often than not religious people and religious organizations that are running the soup kitchens and homeless shelters and refugee resettlement programs, not law professors at fashionable universities with endowments approaching $7 billion." (Sterns 2017, 56).

I like to point out to Christianity's detractors that hospitals, orphanages, the Red Cross, the Salvation Army, public schools, public libraries, to name some of the most obvious, are all the product of Christians and Christian culture. Christianity is concerned about what happens to us when this life is done, but we are also very aware that what happens in this life is important and should be lived well by everyone.

Stern's point is that not only do Christians live in their own peculiar cultural bubble, but those living in various other cultural bubbles around us can be just as obtuse in regards to Christians. The only remedy is to venture across cultural divides to work with and get to know the other side, which is the point of Stern's book.

It is unlikely that Christianity's detractors are looking to search out the true heart of Christianity. Sterns notes one bright spot in Christian vs. the world relations: Kevin Palau and Portland, Oregon. At a time when Sam Adams, an openly gay man, was mayor of Portland, and in a state where Evangelicals had introduced a ballot measure condemning homosexuality, Kevin Palau and the Evangelical community formed an unlikely partnership with Sam Adams and the city of Portland. Kevin, son of famed evangelist Luis Palau, approached Adams about creating a "day of service" for the community. Adams suggested two local schools in desperate need. The "day of service" snowballed into a permanent partnership between hundreds of churches and communities in desperate need (Sterns 2017, 59-68).

It is worth pointing out that most of these churches were from affluent suburbs helping parts of the city that few of them had ever had any connections with prior to this initiative. In other words, it was the Christian community that reached through the bubble of their own Christian community to impact the wider community in a positive way. Adams, a dogged liberal Democrat, saw the energy and enthusiasm of the first day of service and challenged his partners, mostly conservative Republicans, to expand their efforts. He discovered that Christians love to serve their community, for which they earned his continued admiration and gratitude. Those efforts are less likely to receive coverage at

Stern's former employer, National Public Radio, than pedophile priests, but in Portland the impact is substantial. Every city in America should have major active and energetic Christian service outreach until the public impact outweighs the failings of better publicized Christian failures.

Also worth pointing out, this service of the church in Portland is conducted in public institutions, and therefore cannot include proselytizing. The presence of large numbers of Christians in service to the community speaks for itself. The church in Portland has become God's word incarnate. The greatest harm to the body of Christ is when the larger public knows more about aberrations like the Westboro Baptist Church or pedophile priests than they do about the church next door.

The Bubble

The Moonies lived in an extreme cultural bubble caused by their heretical theology, their intense social regimentation, and pressure from churches and the press attacking them on a regular basis. Many of the Christians I associate with these days live in a similar, if not as intense, kind of a cultural bubble owing to a tendency to avoid movies that are not "family value" or Christian movies and music that is not specifically Christian. The result is a cultural isolation that makes it difficult to understand trends in the wider culture.

Christians of the more intense variety, and many of my friends fit that category, tend to speak in jargon. Words like "saved" and "back-slid" have been used enough that many non-believers have some idea of what is meant. Other words, like "fire" or "drunk in the spirit" wouldn't mean anything to many Christians, much less non-Christians.

Moonies worked hard to bridge the gap between their own culture bubble and the wider world. It would be accurate to suggest that Moonies approached all areas of culture with an evangelical zeal. The Moonies had a very active policy of engagement. Through the International Conference on the Unity of the Sciences, which was hosted by Moon, I met Nobel laureates, knighted scientists and other prominent scientists and academics. There is no question that while Moon was being castigated in the press, he was receiving praise from prominent intellectuals.

Additionally, The Congress of World Religions and other programs sponsored by Unification Theological Seminary allowed the church to create bridges to the religious and academic communities.

Despite a dismal entrance into film production with the movie *Inchon*, the Unificationists now have their own movie production company in addition to their publishing company.

I believe that Moon correctly identified the Protestant church's disengagement from the wider culture as a disaster in terms of its ability to influence the direction and growth of culture. He was determined to reverse that trend. The church in America has slowly come to the realization that producing movies from Christian studios is both financially feasible and culturally relevant. The future seems promising.

Enforcing the Borders

Contrary to what the church should be doing, reaching beyond its church bubble, all too often the church is instead hardening the wall around their bubble. I remember, having freshly returned to Christianity, I wanted to find a church for my family. At that time, I worked in the entertainment industry, so I had long hair kept in a pony tail. At several churches we visited, the cold stare of the first greeter told me this church wasn't going to work for me.

The church should open its arms to anyone who wants to come to Jesus. My current church is such a place. For several Sundays we had a young woman who would show up smelling of alcohol and immediately make her way to the front, dancing in a manner not comfortable to normal church culture. During the sermon, she would object loudly, saying God's name is "Jehovah" anytime God was mentioned. The usher would then take her out to the foyer. On one such occasion, I was ushering. I removed her and sat talking with her in the foyer for a long time. In the process, it became clear that she had no interest in Jesus or Christianity, she was just there for the fun of it. She had been welcomed. Sadly, the pastor had to inform her that she must show up clean and sober to be allowed in. The offense wasn't her drinking, or dancing, it was her insistence on being disruptive. As a church, we prayed for that woman and hurt for her. We did our best to welcome her to the house of God just as she was, but in the end, it was clear that her purpose was to disrupt and not to join herself into the body of Christ. Still, we remain a church that will continue to maintain an open attitude to anyone who walks through the door.

As a body, we as Christians must be welcoming to those lost and in need of direction home. In the case of the alcoholic and possibly drug addicted woman, had she been interested, we may have passed her over to a church that was better equipped to handle her special needs. As much as we like to be all things to all people, we are not. The mission of the church must be one of openness, a willingness to engage with all sorts of people, because our purpose is to help them understand how wonderful it is to know Jesus. If the body of Christ isn't open and engaging, but instead builds walls around our Christian enclave, the body of Christ has closed itself to the most important reason why we are here as a body.

Intense Christianity

I have lived in Christian community where daily time with the Lord was expected, as was group prayer and discussions. In some ways, the experience was similar to the Moonie experience, except that Jesus was in the center, and I had a job outside of the community. The community was committed to a deep relationship with Jesus and helping each other to reach spiritual maturity. For me, as a former Moonie, this didn't seem all that radical. For most Christians, this intense Christianity is more than they would care to contemplate. I enjoyed the experience. There are some who come out of addictions, cruel relationships or other life situations for which the only way to become a committed Christian, living a Godly lifestyle, is to pass through a Christian community, a Christian halfway house or similar radical life change. There are some for whom a zealous lifestyle is the only thing comfortable. I know many friends in Christ who were once zealously non- or even anti-Christian, but having changed their ways are now zealously Christian.

On the other hand, there are less intense, more worldly churches. I myself question whether I would be a Christian today without first having become a Moonie. For some, entering the doors of a church is too much for them. Our weekly men's group, that is decidedly not church, honors Jesus and the fellowship of communion. Some of our members are not Christian. Others call themselves Christian, but never attend church. Through us, they have a relationship with Christ, and hopefully they will find themselves growing into a deeper relationship with Christ. The committed Christians of our group are a draw towards a deeper relationship with the body of Christ, and therefore ultimately with Jesus.

One of the problems of the early church was how to deal with Christians who had apostatized themselves owing to persecution. Novatian, a Roman priest of the third century, objected to the election of Cornelius as bishop of Rome because he was too liberal in allowing lapsed Christians back into fellowship. The church leaders met and affirmed Cornelius. Novatian refused to accept the church's decision, so he was excommunicated.

In the fourth through the fifth centuries, a separate group emerged called the Donatists, after the north African bishop

Donatus Magnus, who believed that no apostate priest could be restored to priesthood. Augustine of Hippo argued against Donatism using Christ's parables such as that of the wheat and the tares (Matthew 13:24-30) to claim that we should be careful not to become too rigorous in closing the doors against those who wish to serve the Lord. In the case of Donatism, the church took a more measured approach. The Donatists were condemned by the church in Rome, but in spite of the condemnation, the Donatists were allowed by Rome to continue alongside other Christians for several centuries.

It is fair to suggest that the same sort of sentiment in favor of greater rigor was present with the Pietists and the Puritans. There is a place for communities demanding a higher Christian standard. Some people like to dive into the deep end. However, there are others who will only go in one toe at a time. Most churches offer an open door for them both, as it should be.

Name Your Poison

Every movement in the body of Christ has its extremists, those who go too far. Some, like the Moonies, start out with a belief that places them firmly in the camp of heretics, but most start with an emphasis on some aspect of Christian life such as holiness, faith, baptism, trust in scripture or the gifts of the Spirit which are correct, but then they proceed to push the idea too far.

Let me pick on one example, with apologies to Charles Capps. Although I come from a church which has had a decidedly anti-word faith position, the church, and myself, without fully embracing word-faith, have come to appreciate much that they have to say. I was given a large number of audio files of Charles Capps speaking, and I have come to like him. Because I am a strong advocate for prayer, I picked up a book of Capps on prayer. In a section entitled "Prayer Does Not Change God," he uses Jesus' admonition against vain repetition in prayer (Matthew 6:7) to suggest that God's mind is fixed and repetition won't change it (Capps 1978. 31-34). In other words, Capps is saying pray once, and then expect the answer; do not pray for the same thing again. But, Jesus, in the parable of the persistent widow asks, "will not God give justice to his elect, who cry to him day and night?" The parable is introduced by Luke as a parable "to the effect that they ought always to pray and not lose heart" (Luke 18:1). Going back to the prayer closet over an issue that remains intractable is not the same as vain repetition.

Capps goes on to suggest, "It is not the length of the prayer that moves God. Nor will you be heard for your 'much speaking'. God answers prayer on the legal ground of the new covenant" (Capps 1978. 34). Later, he makes this legal argument even more forcefully: "Prayer is your legal right, but you should come by the rules of spiritual law that govern prayer. Even though you don't, the law will still work–the law says, *he shall have whatsoever he saith*" (Capps 1978. 44). This appears to me to be an instance in which the "word of faith" has become a weird new legal system bordering on Gnosticism. Or, as detractors suggest: "Name it and claim it."

The fact is that Capps was a mighty prayer warrior. He had a great deal to say about faith. But, faith is not the entire gospel. One has to suspect that Capps understood this very well. His book on prayer would not lead me to that conclusion, however.

I don't mean to pick on any one instance of lop-sided theology, but to point out that there are so many aspects to our life in Christ. We can become fixated on only one piece of the puzzle, which will distort the picture, sometimes to our great detriment. This is all a result of living in the bubble where the only voices are positive feedback. I would still recommend Capps to anyone wanting to understand the power of faith. But, on some occasions Capps went a little bit too far. I couldn't recommend his theological acumen.

The Pride of Christ

The Moonies were fighters, not in any physical way, but in prayer and in steady effort to break through the resistance against the church's message. As a Christian, I have retained much of that same fight. I am a strong advocate of prayer, of spiritual warfare, and of continued effort to obtain wisdom and clarity for the church.

As a Moonie, I was spit on, cursed, had a knife pressed to my back, I was detained by the police more than once, and my mother knew how much it cost to have someone "deprogrammed." Through it all, I remained upbeat and positive. I refused to curse those who cursed me. That was Moonie training at work.

As a Christian, my experiences have been less confrontational, so it would seem easier to stay upbeat. On the other hand, so many Christians that I engage with are so very negative about politics, about the economy and about other Christians, including those in our own church. For me, a college graduate trained to think critically, it is far too easy for my thinking to become unnecessarily critical. I'm not tempted to be critical out of meanness, but I really want to find the best way to get things done. The great idea doesn't always give the best results. We have to test our ideas. Ultimately, this can degenerate into the silly mind game of trying to fix things that I can't possibly fix. The mental fight is there for many of us, but often the wisdom is lacking.

I like to think of Christians as the pride of lions that surround the Lion of the Tribe of Judah. We are meant to be the warhorse that Jesus uses to bring down the kingdom of darkness, or more properly to bring the children out of darkness into light. To use Bonhoeffer's terms, "the congregation of Jesus Christ... bears the responsibility for the world" (Bonhoeffer 1955, 318). This is the essential nature of the body of Christ. However, the reality of this Christian life is that all too often we are either couch potatoes for Jesus or we are out there thrashing about without a clue as to how to make our dreams for Jesus become a reality. Worse, our dreams for Jesus are so often nothing but our own personal aspirations with "for Jesus" attached.

In my own case, I can say the issue boils down to not enough prayer, and way too lively flesh. As a Moonie, I got too busy trying to roar in triumph over darkness before the light had illuminated my own personal path. All too often the Church Triumphant appears to be a victory roar of a church with dubious connection to the actual head of the church. As a former Moonie, I can see how easily the apparent humility of the Moonies hid a triumphant belief that the Unificationists were the future kingdom. We had the faith, we really believed, but we were really wrong.

We are called to the field, whichever field that is. We can't wait until we are perfectly dead to self. So, we need to keep ourselves rooted in prayer so that when we are called to action, we hear clearly and are ready to react appropriately. Staying connected to God is the best antidote to foolishness. I would add, that if you can't listen to criticism without becoming angry and aggressively defensive, you have failed humility 101. It might be worthwhile to calmly reevaluate the criticism.

Is It OK to Turn the Faucet

One reporter, telling of his experience at a Moonie weekend retreat, said he had gotten to the point where he questioned whether it was acceptable to turn on the water or not. This is not an issue with the Moonies only. Any intense Christian community can get a person to the point that every breath has to be for the Lord. I have heard countless sermons suggesting that a failure to witness is a failure to be Christian and that saving souls is the one essential work of Christianity. This is a trap of the devil. It puts the Christian back in the position of self analyzing and judging. We have already covered this as a return to the Fall, eating from the forbidden fruit. It may be that your destiny is to evangelize the world, but it may just as well be that your kingdom destiny is to provide an environment that transforms an industry, or maybe you are the one tasked with raising tomorrow's world changer.

Jesus Christ is not concerned with the color of your socks, and it is completely acceptable to take time to relax, to play, to do the things that non-Christians do. Listening to non-Christian music is not a sin. Watching a non-Christian movie is not a sin. There are both music and movies that challenge our relationship with Christ in a bad way. A Christian should be able to tell the difference. I was given a blues CD that had G.. D... inserted into every line. I like the blues, and I really like the person who gave it to me, but I pitched the CD in the trash without listening to the whole album. The one who gave it to me had never heard it. He just wanted to bless me with something he thought I would like.

Bonhoeffer goes further. He suggests that we belong in the world because the world belongs to Jesus Christ. It is our job to love the world enough to bring it to Jesus. For Bonhoeffer, this is what it means to take responsibility for the world. It is not dressing ourselves in super-spirituality, but being real people in the hands of Christ, doing real worldly things in complete submission to Jesus. "The reality of God discloses itself only by setting me entirely in the reality of the world, and when I encounter the reality of the world it is already sustained, accepted and reconciled in the reality of God" (Bonhoeffer 1955, 193). You and I carry the light of heaven into the world.

CHAPTER FIFTEEN

HEALING THE WORLD

Marriages

The Unification Church saw every failure of humankind as something that could be repaired. However naive their approach was, they were willing to put everything on the line to change things. Moonies were fully engaged on every level, from politics to the arts, from academia to religious dialogue, but nowhere is their commitment to change more profound than in marriage.

Moonies are perhaps best known for their mass weddings. Thousands of couples were married in large stadium events. The first to receive international notoriety was a ceremony in Madison Square Garden of more than 2000 couples. This was the 1982 wedding that I was meant to take part in, had I not left the church.

Mass weddings are a little odd, but odder yet for modern westerners is the practice of matching couples. Sun Myung Moon not only personally matched couples, but he commonly matched couples across racial and ethnic boundaries, often with the express purpose of healing the divisions between people. Wikipedia quotes one of my former classmates, Frank Kaufmann, who went on to lead a Moonie sponsored ecumenical organization:

> We do not have mass weddings because Reverend
> Moon doesn't know any better, doesn't know
> how Americans react to things, or that he
> stubbornly adheres to some odd Korean habit.
> Our matchings and weddings are a direct and
> perfect manifestation of a profound theology and
> world view. You see, Unificationists believe that
> all the problems on Earth, from the Gulf War,
> to child abuse, to the crumbling school system
> (you name it) are fruits of the fact that self-interest
> crept into the family, the love between husband
> and wife, reproductive affairs, and parent-child
> relationships, thus since the beginning there has
> never been even one family whose members were
> not dominated by some significant degree of self-
> interest (Kaufmann 2019).

Notice that Kaufman seems to be pointing directly to "self-interest" in relationships as the root issue. Unwittingly, Kaufmann is undercutting the Unificationist argument that the root of evil is unsanctioned sex rather than the root of evil being a personal viewpoint separate from God's viewpoint. I don't know if Moon's solution is helping to change things, but one has to admire the willingness of Moonies to take the leap of marrying across racial and ethnic fault lines.

In 1988, Moon matched 6500 Korean and Japanese together in an effort to heal the historical rifts between the two countries. Japan has invaded Korea many times over the centuries, with resulting racial animosity. Many couples Moon matched didn't even speak a common language.

Moonies claim an above normal success rate for their marriages, although there are no hard statistics to prove their claims. Since high ideals and self-sacrifice are at the heart of Moonie doctrine, it is not impossible to believe that they are having greater success than the typical marriage. Anecdotally, I would say that many of the married couples in the Unification Church struggle with many of the same issues that most married couples do. However, these couples, referred to internally as "Blessed Couples," have a nearly sacred status in the church. During my time in the Unification Church there really was no way to leave the relationship outside of leaving the church. This provides social pressure reminiscent of older Christian values.

Moon's first wife left him and therefore his still fledgling church. There was a second wife who was apparently raped by the North Korean soldiers during the Korean War. The implication of the story is that she was no longer suitable to be the wife of the Lord of the Second Advent. Exactly what happened to that wife was never clear to me. And then there is Nansook Hong the wife of Moon's eldest son by his third and final wife, who left amid accusations of abuse. High ideals don't necessarily provide the rich fruit we hope for.

Moonies and the World

Moonies did have high ideals. The one thing at the heart of Unificationism that is commendable is that desire to bridge boundaries, to unite, to bring an end to long standing conflict. Of course, everyone wants peace, love and happiness. On the other hand, there are a lot of people who work very hard to create conflict, thinking that conflict brings healthy change. Part of ending conflict is identifying those who are actively creating conflict.

I spent some of my time with the Moonies working in an anti-Communism project, Freedom Leadership Foundation. I researched Communist organizations and exposed the principles of Communism in and around Chicago. One thing that became painfully clear is that Communists are professionals at identifying social subgroups and setting them at odds with the larger society. In other words, they were creating animosity between people groups. The more violent the better. Communist organizing was at direct odds with everything that the Unification Church stood for. In Japan, where the Communists had a significant presence, this led to some violent clashes between Moonies and Communists. In my case, my confrontations were more comical than troubling.

I took several church members to counter-demonstrate at a Communist demonstration outside of the Standard Oil building in Chicago. I approached an officer who seemed to be in charge and asked where we should set up. He pointed to the barricades where the Communists were busy shouting and waving placards. I said that might not be a good idea and repeated we were anti-Communism. He was surprised and hastily organized a separate barricade for us. Our photos were taken by Communists, who assured us that we would be the first eliminated after the revolution.

I don't know that my year with Freedom Leadership Foundation produced any tangible results, but it was certainly an eye opener into the world of left-wing extremism. I flinch when I hear the term "progressive" now. Many Marxist front groups were using that same label at the time. It seems the current Marxist fashion is to label themselves Antifa, as if provoking violent clashes with the extreme right was socially helpful.

The Unification Church's anti-Communism got them involved with groups like the Contras in Nicaragua and the Mujahidin in Afghanistan. The church's connections with the Contras got them involved in the "Contragate" affair under the Reagan administration. Several of Moon's top confidants served as middle men between the Contras and the administration. Bo Hi Pak, Moon's right-hand man, and others close to Moon were called to testify before Congress. The Unification Church was also suspected of involvement in the "Koreagate" affair, which involved cash payments to congressmen in order to reverse President Richard Nixon's decision to remove US troops from South Korea. To my knowledge that suspicion was never proved. Normally the church would have been more likely to take out a full page ad against removing troops, or to hold large outdoor rallies rather than to bribe public officials.

One of my last assignments with the church was to work for its educational branch creating video teaching material. Shortly after I left the Unification Church, my good friend and colleague Lee Shapiro went to Nicaragua, where he was able to embed with Contra resistance fighters during their civil war. He released the documentary film *Nicaragua Was Our Home* in 1986. The film was shown on some PBS stations and at the Sundance Film Festival. The film was heavily critical of the leftist Sandinista government and their ties to Cuba, which squared well with the church's anti-Communism. He and another colleague were killed in Afghanistan while filming resistance to the Soviet occupation there in 1987. These two former colleagues of mine died trying to shed light on current issues.

Christians and the World

It seems that most Christian engagement concerning social issues has been reactive, usually trying to shut the door long after the horse has left the barn. This has been the situation with gay rights, sexual liberation, drug culture and the arts. The result is that the appearance of Christians in general is bumbling, out-of-touch and anti-everything. There are some excellent Christian academic and arts leaders, but they need forums to showcase their art and ideas. It seems that in most contemporary arts and academic showcases, the Christian artists and academics are the odd man out. Many of them either intentionally or by the habits of their profession down play their Christian roots.

There are some efforts to turn things around. Sherwood Films, with successful films directed at Christian audiences, has definitely given Hollywood a reason to re-evaluate. I refuse to believe that it is too late. The Mars Hill Audio Journal showcases Christian authors, both academic and cultural. Many of these have significant things to say about current cultural trends, but all too often have very few places to get their ideas out to a larger public.

Makoto Fujimura, discussed above, is also an author of books such as *Culture Care (Fujimura 2017)*, which infuses a Christian ethical approach into the arts: "Our keys are humility, integrity, determination, and hope for things to come. In the current art world in which ego, selfishness, and self-destruction abound, we will stand out, eventually, if we have an ounce of human decency and generosity" *(Fujimura 2017, 110-111)*.

Christians are meant to bring peace and healing. The arts is one of our most significant levers to move things in God's manner. All too often Christians spend their time deciding who is the repugnant cultural other instead. "When we 'win' culture war battles by demonizing the other side, the resulting paralysis and disappointments lead to the expanse of fissures rather than the soil of abundance" *(Fujimura 2017, 129)*.

Sanctuary

Since the rise of monasticism, the church has been known as a place of sanctuary. The Unification Church, in my day, was a place where you were either all in... or you were out. So, it could offer no sanctuary except full membership in the group. While fundraisers often used lines like, "We are raising funds to get youth off of drugs," what they meant was that they were raising funds to make church members of young people.

Churches are some of the biggest and best sponsors of sanctuary services: crisis shelters, Alcoholics Anonymous,

Narcotics Anonymous, refugee resettlement, soup kitchens and homeless shelters, as well as outreach to shut-ins and the elderly, to name the few that come immediately to mind. Many Christians actively engage in these activities. But, many Christians prefer to keep some distance between themselves and those in need of sanctuary from this world's cruelty. Sanctuary is the place where people come who have become soiled by this world's ills. Cleaning up messy lives is a big part of sanctuary.

I don't think Christians are unique in their dislike of life's messes. To their credit, many Christians are the first to step into those uncomfortable places. Christians know that financial support for services to those in need is essential. We also understand that sometimes what is needed most is a warm embrace, someone to listen without judgment, or someone that can be called when the monkey is on the back. Being that someone is sometimes hard.

The Unification Church that I knew was young and enthusiastic, but had none of the maturity needed for dealing with life's crises. It was not a place of sanctuary. Most Moonies were well educated and came from good homes, but were unprepared to confront lives in crisis.

CHAPTER SIXTEEN

Big Tuna

Part of the Team

From the first, being a Moonie was a challenge. Despite having graduated college with a degree in theater, I was never comfortable engaging strangers. I was a scene designer and technical director, enjoying the anonymity of staying back stage and working in the shadows.

Raw recruits to the Unification Church were immediately absorbed into the group, living in community and working as a team. As mentioned, I was quickly put out on the street and forced to confront total strangers in the hopes of engaging them for the cause. I viewed it all as a personal challenge to become a more outgoing person. My time as a Moonie definitely gave me more confidence for public speaking and general social interaction.

The church was very big on setting higher and higher goals for itself and for each individual member. So, for instance, on a fund-raising team each member would set a personal goal of so many dollars to raise. I usually set a $100 goal. Anything less was viewed as a too low a target. I rarely got anywhere near my goal, which was demoralizing. I worked as hard as possible, stayed as bright and positive as possible, but was always close to the bottom in results.

Results did count in the church. While I was in seminary, it came to light that some of the fundraising team were using wheelchairs as a tactic to elicit sympathy. I believe this started when an injured fundraiser was forced to use one and discovered that it proved successful. In any case, several of us felt strongly that it was highly unethical to use a wheelchair if the individual didn't need one, but we had no way to get our disagreement up the chain of command. However, during summer break, the seminarians were sent out on fundraising teams as a personal challenge exercise. One of the seminarians managed to reach the top fund raiser status. This gave him the ability to raise the question of ethics and to be heard. The practice was immediately banned.

Exotic Adventure

Personal challenge and character building were seen as a goal in the Unification Church. This was the time when the Peace Corps was still popular. A group called Outward Bound was setting up outdoor education schools here in the United States. Their stated purpose was and still is that of character building and strengthening self-confidence, usually through outdoor adventures. A less strenuous equivalent would be a ropes course.

Sun Myung Moon was interested in developing a similar sort of program, starting with the seminarians, who were meant to be the Moonie elites. Moon liked to fish. He arrived at the seminary one sunny morning with fishing nets. Unification Theological Seminary sits on the banks of the Hudson River, which happens to be loaded with carp, an invasive species of oriental fish. There is a nearby shallow lagoon along the banks of the Hudson River. The students were all sent into the water dragging the nets with the intention of catching carp. Moon sat with his wife in a row boat overseeing the whole adventure. We came up dismally empty.

Moon did not accept defeat or embarrassment. Under his direction, we took the nets up to the soccer field where every afternoon after classes the seminarians were put to work repairing and stitching the nets together into one very long net. I had been a Sea Scout and knew my knots, so I became the net expert. Others were sent down to the lagoon to mark out the low tide mark with poles. When ready, the net was taken down to the lagoon and stretched between the poles at high tide. We then waited for low tide. When the tide went out, thousands of carp were stranded behind the nets in muddy pools.

At this point, the sensible thing would have been to release the carp. Instead we gathered them up and put them in an old swimming pool on the seminary grounds. We did our best to keep them alive while leadership decided what to do with them. One of my interesting, but less glamorous jobs, was diving into a pool full of thousands of fish to scoop the dead ones off the bottom so we could take them and bury them in the woods. I have always been outdoorsy, having grown up in Alaska, so this sort of thing wasn't difficult for me. Swimming in a pool with thousands of carp is a unique experience.

Eventually, some of the small colorful ones were placed in a very large fish tank in the seminary, while the rest were transported in a dump truck full of water to a lake in a subdivision where many of the church leaders owned homes. By this time, Moon had already determined to greatly expand the pond at the seminary. He wanted the seminarians to dig it by hand. After draining the pond and a month of backbreaking digging on our part, it was concluded that it would take a half a century to complete the project. Heavy equipment was brought in to finish the work.

Outward Bound

After seminary, I spent a year as the state leader of Wisconsin. Then, I returned to New York to join a newly formed production team creating educational material for the church. That summer the seminarians were sent to Gloucester, Massachusetts, for a tuna fishing adventure consciously based on the Outward Bound model. Although I had already graduated, our team joined the adventure to chronicle the fishing and create a film based on the effort.

The Unification Church is rooted in Korea, but has a strong presence in Japan, where Moon went to school. Moon knew that the price of bluefin tuna, bluefin sashimi being a prized delicacy in Japan, was very much higher in Tokyo than in the U.S. He had started manufacturing small fishing boats that were about 20 feet long in a New York plant. They resembled a Boston Whaler, but used a triple hull design. The church also purchased a fish packing plant in Gloucester. The plant began packing whole tuna on ice and air freighting them to Tokyo. This doubled the price of the fish at the dock in Gloucester.

It seemed like a win-win situation to marry a successful business model with the Outward Bound model, so we set out to catch tuna. The local fishermen were less than enthusiastic about all the new competition from a dozen new boats. When the Moonies sent out a boat with an all-female crew; this so upset some of the locals that they rammed their boat trying to get them off the water.

It turns out that fishing for bluefin tuna is long and tedious work. It involves setting out several baited hooks, spaced at intervals and descending into the depths. The idea is to cut up mackerel and pitch the pieces into the water so that they drift down past the hooks into the depths below. This setup was meant to get the tuna to follow this column of "chum" up from below until they swallow a baited hook. That summer, things were going at a slow pace. Some of the fishermen had been out all summer and had nothing to show for it. I remember cutting up fish hour after hour, watching the chum drift down into the dark below. We fished commercial style. The hooks were on steel leaders attached to the end of a very long hemp rope, with floats attached at variable distances from the hook so that the hooks would step down into the depths. We had to endlessly adjust the set of the baited hooks so they stayed in the downward drift of the chum. We also had to check the hooks periodically to make sure that sharks hadn't stolen the bait. The process involved hours of concentration in the midst of monotony.

The first day out, we were all sea sick. We anchored in the dark to be ready to drop our lines at sunrise. There we were, all day in a tiny boat bobbing up and down until our stomach felt like a washing machine stuck in the wash cycle. On top of that, we were cutting up dead fish under a bright sun all day long. We used aircraft cable for the leaders and spliced loops into them rather than using the standard crimps. Experience told our team that the tuna jerk hard enough to occasionally break the aircraft cable at the crimps, so splicing and whipping down the splice was more reliable. The hemp was carefully coiled in a plastic wash basket. Once the line was fed out to the desired length, it was clipped with a clothes pin. This served two purposes. One, it kept the line from pulling more length out of the basket. But, more importantly, when a tuna hit the hook and jerked back, the line would pop out of the clip with a distinct snap. The important thing to know is that Atlantic bluefin tuna are big. They start at 350 pounds. I was successful in that I was there for three separate catches. All were over 900 pounds, the third was 1024 pounds. That is why aircraft cable is used for leaders.

Snap! After days in the sleepy doldrums of nothing, that sound brings the boat to full alert. One fisherman grabs the line, which is already flying out of the basket at incredible speed. Another puts on fighting gloves to prevent rope burns and immediately takes over. These gloves have plastic similar to hot glue in patterns across them to allow the rope to slide without catching, but providing sufficient friction to slow the fish down. The rest of the crew would release the anchor onto a float and pull in all the other lines as fast as possible so they wouldn't become tangled with the racing line that had our prize on the end. Now the fight is on.

Since you have been anchored in a packed fleet of boats at a corner of the continental shelf, the idea is to encourage the angry fish to pull the boat into open water away from the other boats. You tug hard if the fish veers towards other boats and you let him run if he heads for open water. With the boat now off its anchor, the fish pulls the boat behind him. This is what the old whalers referred to as a Nantucket sleigh ride.

Once in open water, the crew has to tire the fish out until it can be pulled in close enough to be harpooned. Two fishermen at a time would work the fish, one to pull on the rope and one to keep the coil on the deck from getting tangled. When the fish runs toward the boat, the line has to be laid down very fast and very neatly because when the fish turns around, the rope can be playing out so fast it jumps off the deck. I watched a local with a catch who had a young helper who was doing a poor job of line tending. The fisherman was jumping and screaming curses trying to stay out of the line dancing off the deck. If your foot is tangled in a line with an very upset 900 pound fish on the other end, the results can be deadly. This fight with the tuna can take hours before the fish is close enough to harpoon.

The harpoons we used were hand thrown harpoons, not much different from the old-fashioned whaling harpoons with the tip that released and stayed in the fish. A line was attached to pull the fish in. The heavy wooden shaft was then pulled in separately. When the harpoon had done its work and the tuna was killed, the fish would be pulled alongside the boat. The tuna would be too large for us to lift into our small boats, so after pulling in the catch they would be lashed to the side for the ride back to the dock.

Overfishing of bluefin tuna has seriously depleted fishing stocks, leading to tougher regulations on fishing. Whether the church's Outward Bound experiment was able to continue or not, I don't know. My suspicion is that environmental concerns have made it untenable.

The Mountain Top

I remember a question and answer session held at the seminary with the then president of the Unification Church in the U.S. One seminarian questioner implied that the current membership was not the best of the best. The answer from then president Neil Albert Salonen was simple, "We called from the mountain top, and this is who came."

Most commentators have had the opposite opinion from that of my fellow seminarian. Moonies generally seemed to be bright, intelligent and well educated. I believe that the theology of the church appealed to educated people with slightly new age leanings. It took them from the existential angst of most colleges to a hopeful eye on creating a better future. More than that, the Unification Church, and Moon in particular, consciously worked to bring out the best in people. The tuna fishing and other challenges may not seem to be normal church activities, but they were intentionally designed to develop the best people possible.

The development of leadership skills and personal challenge should be a part of all churches with the ability to provide these services, especially for young adults. Encouraging academic excellence is important, but creating Christian leaders takes more than a college degree.

CHAPTER SEVENTEEN

GOD'S SABBATH

In Christ

I have tried to show, and have used Bonhoeffer, Richardson and Edwards to reinforce the point, good works are not the core of Christianity. At the same time, I hope I have shown that Christians are, and should always be, leaders in doing good works because of who they are in Christ. Being a good person is not Christianity. But all Christians should be, or at least be becoming, good people. Bonhoeffer is especially clear that moral behavior, for the Christian, comes from our nearness to Jesus Christ and not from any other moral yardstick. This, I believe, is why the Unificationists still can't get it right, despite all the good they are engaged in.

Salvation is the first step to a new life in Jesus Christ. The most essential ingredient of continued Godly life is the Holy Spirit. In the Old Testament, the Spirit fell on a few individuals here and there. Following the death and resurrection of Jesus, on the day of Pentecost, the Spirit fell on the entire gathering (Acts 2:1-4). Even up to this point, the evidence of the Spirit was only seen among the Jews, but in chapter 10 of the Book of Acts, the apostle Peter has a vision while in prayer. The Holy Spirit tells him to follow a group of gentile visitors. Peter finds himself speaking to a gathering at the house of a non-Jew, a gentile, and to a large group of gentiles he has gathered. As Peter is testifying of Jesus, "To him all the prophets bear witness that everyone who believes in him receives forgiveness of sins through his name" (Acts 10:43), a remarkable thing happens:

> While Peter was still saying these things, the Holy Spirit fell on all who heard the word. And the believers from among the circumcised who had come with Peter were amazed, because the gift of the Holy Spirit was poured out even on the Gentiles. For they were hearing them speaking in tongues and extolling God. Then Peter declared, "Can anyone withhold water for baptizing these people, who have received the Holy Spirit just as we have?" And he commanded them to be baptized in the name of Jesus Christ (Acts 10:44-48).

The Jews had a very low view of the spiritual potential of any non-Jew. The circumstances of this event are so dramatic that Peter is forced to explain himself to the church back in Jerusalem, even though he is the leader and spokesman of the church (Acts 11:1-18).

Fire from Heaven

Now what this means in practice for believers today varies greatly between the many doctrines and cultures of modern believers. I do not intend to open that can of worms. I want to stick with what we should all be able to agree on. I love the Catholics, the Calvinists, the Arminians and the Pentecostals, and I am sure that God is using them all. Let me start by repeating a quote from Jonathan Edwards, who is anything but Pentecostal:

The sum of the blessings Christ sought, by what
he did and suffered in the work of redemption was
the Holy Spirit (Edwards 2004, 55).

Edwards did not believe in speaking in tongues, or faith
healing, or other signs, but he did see heaven move.

In 1734, God began to move in the American colonies.
Edwards was privileged to be instrumental in what he called a
harvest, or awakening. Pastor friends of his in Scotland wanted
more detail, so Edwards composed a very long letter in 1736. His
friends went in haste to London taking the letter to a publisher.
The resulting book, *A Narrative of the Revival of Religion in New
England* is 155 pages (Edwards 1829). The book became an instant
success in Britain and Europe.

George Whitefield and the Wesley brothers had begun
successful evangelical campaigns in England, and Whitefield
was inspired to come to the colonies in 1740. His arrival fanned
the flames of revival known as the Great Awakening. But,
revival is a messy affair. Waves of ecstatic enthusiasm offended
the conservative establishment. Worse, there were reports
of untrained and unordained preachers starting churches in
the western wilderness. Some of these fell into teachings and
behaviors that fell far outside of accepted Christian practice.
There were reports of outlandish behavior and heretical
teachings. As a result, an influential Boston preacher wrote a
book condemning the Awakening. When Whitefield returned
for a second tour of the colonies, he found very few pulpits open
to him and had to preach in the open air. The ardor had cooled
considerably.

Edwards responded with several works, including *Some
Thoughts Concerning the Present Revival of Religion in New
England* (Edwards 1829) and *A Treatise Concerning the Religious
Affections* (Edwards 1999). Edwards who disapproved of frivolous
laughter or levity on Sundays, never-the-less presents a balanced

defense of religious enthusiasm. For Edwards, high emotions have to be expected when God touches the heart. But, he declares:

> I don't mean, however, that the more emotional you are, the more spiritual you'll be. Even true saints experience emotions that are not spiritual; their emotions are often mixed, some from grace, much from nature... The degree of our spirituality should be judged more by the strength of our emotional habit, rather than by the temporary emotions that come and go, moment by moment (Edwards 1999).

Edwards lived in a time of hellfire and brimstone preaching. He is perhaps best known for his sermon, "Sinners in the Hands of an Angry God" (Edwards 1741). But it is his understanding of the beauty of knowing God that sets him above his contemporaries. For Edwards, the arrival of the Holy Spirit is the arrival of true grace:

> True grace is not an inactive thing; in fact, nothing in heaven and earth is more active, for grace is life itself, spiritual and divine life. It is not a barren thing, for nothing in the universe is more fruitful (Edwards 1999).

A New Religious Paradigm

In 1995, Harvey Cox wrote his book *Fire From Heaven*. Not only could he not avoid the fact that religion was not disappearing as he and many other pundits and scholars predicted (Cox 1995, 103), but we were in the midst of an upsurge of a very raw religious expression, not unlike the Great Awakening that so disturbed the religious establishment of its day. He begins his book with the story of the abject failure of the 1893 *World Parliament of Religions*, part of the Columbia Exposition in Chicago. The parliament featured debates between Christian apologists and representatives of other world religions. Hindu apologists were perceived to have won the day. The exposition featured a Great White City appearing to be made of marble, but actually made of jute and plaster. It burned to the ground not long after the close of the exposition.

This was followed a decade later by a Pentecostal revival on Azusa Street, which was on the "colored" side of Los Angeles. The Azusa Street revival was led by the one-eyed son of a former slave:

> Azusa street was raw, stormy, plainly American in its tactlessness and lack of refinement. The contrast reveals a fissure that has always tormented the American psyche. The architectural historian M. Christine Boyer believes that the Beaux-Arts architects who laid out the White City did everyone a calamitous disservice. Rather than embracing the real energies of the American city and then moving ahead, they created instead a halfbreed, splicing "the civic ideals and ceremonial urbanities of the European city" onto the American town. But almost the same words could be written about the American theology of the day. It was the beginning of the period of obsequious deference to German scholarship, when George Wilhelm Hegel and Friedrich Schleiermacher eclipsed Americans like Jonathan Edwards and Ralph Waldo Emerson in the divinity schools (Cox 1995, 29-30).

Unwittingly, Cox has brought us back to Richardson's argument that the secular city is desperate for a new authentic expression of Christianity, an American theology. "Perhaps modern, liberal western theology—the kind I learned as a graduate student—has been vainly striving to reconcile religion to an allegedly scientific worldview which is actually becoming more outdated every day" (Cox 1995, 258). As churches tied to liberal theology continue to shrink, a religion of "primal spirituality" is exploding worldwide (Cox 1995, 82).

Humility and Unity

Edwards book on *The Religious Affections* deals with two forms of humility: legal and evangelical humility (Edwards 1999, 193). Remember he had seen great revival, but much of it was lost in later years. He is deeply concerned with what went wrong. "Legal" humility comes when the Spirit is at work in the natural world to bring about a change of heart. This could be incredible worship, great preaching or signs and wonders. "Evangelical" humility is caused by "the Spirit's supernatural influence, when He implants divine seeds within the human heart" (Edwards 1999, 193).

> When people are humbled from a legalistic point of view, they may be aware that God is great and terrible, but they do not know how much they need Him; they still see themselves as the center of their universe, and they have no impulse to surrender themselves to God in worship and love. This impulse is given only when we experience evangelical humility, for then our hearts are overcome; we no longer seek only ourselves, for we have seen God's holy beauty (Edwards 1999, 194).

Edwards is speaking of "primal spirituality", yet he would not understand much of what Cox is describing. The secular city that Cox describes is a city of turbulence and chaos, one that encourages a retreat into cultural enclaves. Each enclave is its own feedback loop, encouraging self-centered thought. In the midst of it, who doesn't want something more? Azusa Street represents a whirlwind that cut through distinctions of class, and race, and nationality. "God shows no partiality" (Acts 10:34). Thirty-eight missionaries left to spread the message within the first six months of the mission's life (Cox 1995, 101-102). Even though the mission only lasted a few years, the effect has been felt worldwide.

The spirit of unity that marked the Azusa Street revival did not last. Very soon there were defections, even in the midst of a unity that was clearly inspired of evangelical humility. Several pastors left to form their own Pentecostal denominations. I can't help but think that the very same legal humility that Edwards points out was at work in their midst. Having seen an astounding work of the Spirit, many began to think themselves keepers of greater understanding than anyone else. "But the person who habitually assumes that she is spiritually superior to others is really no saint at all" (Edwards 1999, 211). Intellectual pursuit without the vision of a wonderful and terrible God fuels discord over all sorts of lesser issues.

Herbert Richardson's book *Toward an American Theology* includes a chapter on "A Philosophy of Unity" (Richardson 1967, 71-107). It is a heady discussion, but his understanding of unity rests on one thing: God, in all His aspects, "And he is before all things, and in him all things hold together" (Colossians 1:17).

> If we can see the beauty of holiness, then we are seeing the thing most essential to the world... Unless we understand this, all other learning merely wastes the intellect God gave us (Edwards 1999, 157-8).

The church that I am a part of is a wild and crazy charismatic church, but we have learned to behave ourselves when across the street at the Methodist church or down the road at the Baptist or Presbyterian churches. We work well with them because fundamentally we recognize there are things we do well, and things we don't. In fact, there are things that some of those other Christians do very much better than we do. We all work much better as a team. I believe God is delighted to see us work together. "Behold, how good and pleasant it is when brothers dwell in unity" (Psalms 133:1)!

We have theological disagreements, for sure, but, as Edwards notes, "The early church never required a written exam as part of their initiation process. They did require a profession of the things the Spirit had done—but they never insisted on a theological understanding of just how the spirit accomplished these things" (Edwards 1999, 285).

The New Face of Christianity

"Spirit filled" churches are rapidly growing, while older denominations continue to shrink. It is not that all other forms of Christianity are doomed to disappear. Rather, the Pentecostals, the Charismatics and others have done a better job of voicing a vision of God that is the answer to the religious angst of the secular city. The Christianity of Azusa Street was born mostly devoid of intellectual and cultural demands.

Unfortunately, this does not mean that they are any more God-directed than their predecessors. It is very easy to conform to a "Spirit filled" culture, to fall out in the Spirit, to make ecstatic utterances, to prophesy, to shake or to war in the Spirit, but still be just as self-centered as ever. Lack of doctrinal substructure in Charismatic churches can lead to serious deviation from biblical Christianity. This is particularly prevalent in churches which exclude themselves from fellowship with other churches and Christian gatherings.

Cox put his finger on the golden ring, when he suggested that "primal spirituality" seemed to be what this world is craving. This is nothing new, but the urgency of it is much greater in this world we live in. "Religion" has become a bad word, even in church. Why? Because it has come to represent the affectation of genuine spirituality. We all understand this, but there is no church where there are no tares among the wheat. There have always been and will always be, at least until Christ returns, those who have learned how to fake the signs of spirituality. Even more confusing is that often these same individuals have their moments of genuine spirituality.

The key to the strength of the church and the validity of the Christian message in this day is the promotion of a strong prayer culture. My friends and I pray for people in public regularly. We pray simple, direct prayers. Nothing flowery. In Walmart, it is best to be subdued. This is a private transaction between the one praying, the one being prayed for and God. Everyone has needs. A good prayer of primal spirituality is to ask God to help with the need. We pray for people who prefer witchcraft to Christianity, and we pray for Christians. Prayer is a universal language of blessing.

That same attitude toward simple, direct prayer is how I pray at home, in church, or with friends. For myself, I would rather offend someone than allow them to dominate prayer time with flowery preaching. Prayer is a transaction between the one praying, the need and God. I cannot imagine calling for the presence of the God of all creation, only to turn my back on Him to read off my laundry list of what I think everyone else present should be doing, even if presented as a prayer. Prayer is a time to hand God the keys to the car and say, "would You please take the wheel. I don't think I can do this without You."

The other essential ingredient to primal spirituality is unity. We achieve unity with others when we listen to them, share with them, spend time with them. We have unity with God in prayer. We get unity with the law and the prophets, Jesus and the apostles when we read the Bible and meditate on it. And, we achieve unity with the other churches in our community when we join them in prayer services, work projects, or just supporting their special events. Unity cuts through all the layers of culture and dogma and exposes the common thread in the midst of all of Christianity, our relation to God the Father, Christ Jesus and the Holy Spirit. That is where the church started, and it is still the backbone of the body of Christ. Hearing from heaven, we are alive in Christ. Any form of Christian service, or post-Christian service that is not connected to God are dead works (Hebrews 6:1).

The secular city does not have a solution. It is constantly churning out reformers with doomsday scenarios, and social critics who are pointing to this or that evil influence. The secular city is not a melting pot, it is a stew with all sorts of lumps in hot broth. Only the creator God is able to hold it all in His hand, in His love. The purpose of the church is to reveal that gospel.

> until we all attain to the unity of the faith and of the knowledge of the Son of God, to mature manhood, to the measure of the stature of the fullness of Christ, so that we may no longer be children, tossed to and fro by the waves and carried about by every wind of doctrine, by human cunning, by craftiness in deceitful schemes. Rather, speaking the truth in love, we are to grow up in every way into him who is the head, into Christ, from whom the whole body, joined and held together by every joint with which it is equipped, when each part is working properly, makes the body grow so that it builds itself up in love (Ephesians 4:13- 16).

BIBLIOGRAPHY

A-C

Altizer, Thomas J.J. 1966. *Radical Theology and the Death of God.* Indianapolis, IN: Bobbs-Merrill Company.

Barnes, Albert. 1834. *Notes on the Bible.* In the public domain. Widely available online and included in most Bible study software.

Barnes, Rebecca and Lindy Lowry. "7 Startling Facts: An Up Close Look at Church Attendance in America." *Outreach Magazine.* April 10, 2018. Accessed January 18, 2019. https://churchleaders. com/pastors/ pastor-articles/139575-7-startling-facts-an-up-close-look-at-church-attendance-in-america.html.

Berger, Peter L. and Thomas Luckmann. 1966. *The Social Construction of Reality: A Treatise on the Sociology of Knowledge.* Garden City, NY: Doubleday.

Berger, Peter L. 1967. *The Sacred Canopy: Elements of a Sociological Theory of Religion.* Garden City, NY: Doubleday & Company, Inc.

Bonhoeffer, Dietrich. 1954. *Life Together.* Translated by John W. Doberstein. San Francisco, CA: Harper & Row, Publishers.

Bonhoeffer, Dietrich. 1955. *Ethics.* Translated by Neville Horton Smith. NY: Touchstone Books (1995).

Bonhoeffer, Dietrich. 1959. *The Cost of Discipleship.* Translated by R. H. Fuller, with revision by Irmgard Booth. NY: Touchstone Books (1995).

Bonhoeffer, Dietrich. 1966. *Christ the Center*. Translated by John Bowden. NY: Harper & Row, Publishers.

Bonhoeffer, Dietrich. 1967. *Letters and Papers from Prison. Revised Edition*. Edited by Eberhard Bethge. Translated by Reginald Fuller and revised by Frank Clarke and others. NY: The Macmillan Company.

Boslooper, Thomas. 1962. *The Virgin Birth*. Philadelphia, PA: The Westminster Press.

Capps, Charles. 1978. *Releasing the Ability of God Through Prayer*. England, AR: Capps Publishing.

Childe, V. Gordon. 1936. *Man Makes Himself*. NY: New American Library (1951).

Clarke, Adam. 1831. *Adam Clarke's Commentary on the Bible*. Originally published in six volumes. In the public domain. Widely available online and included in most Bible study software.

Cobb, John B. & David Roy Griffin. 1976. *Process Theology*. Philadelphia, PA: The Westminster Press.

Cox, Harvey. 1973. *The Seduction of the Spirit: The Use and Misuse of the People's Religion*. NY: Simon & Schuster.

Cox, Harvey. 1977. *Turning East: The Promise and Peril of the New Orientalism*. London: Allen Lane, Penguin Books, Ltd.

Cox, Harvey. 1984. *Religion in the Secular City: Toward a Post-Modern Theology*. NY: Simon & Schuster.

Cox, Harvey. 1995. *Fire from Heaven; The Rise of Pentecostal Spirituality and the Reshaping of Religion in the Twenty-first Century*. Reading, MA: Addison-Wesley Publishing Company.

Cox, Harvey. 2013. *The Secular City: Secularization and Urbanization in Theological Perspective*. Princeton, NJ: Princeton University Press. Originally published in 1965. This 48th anniversary edition includes a new introduction by the author, as well as the author's introduction to the 25th anniversary edition.

D-G

Dorrien, Gary. 2001. *The Making of American Liberal Theology: Imagining Progressive Religion, 1805 – 1900.* Quoted in: Kevin DeYoung "Seven Characteristics of Liberal Theology" September 26, 2017. *The Gospel Coalition.* Accessed: February 9, 2019. https://www.thegospelcoalition.org/blogs/kevin-deyoung/seven-characteristics-of-liberal-theology/.

DP. 1973. *Divine Principle.* NY: Holy Spirit Association for the Unification of World Christianity. There is no author listed. Young Oon Kim translated the Korean text to English in 1973. According to Dr. Kim, who was a professor at Unification Theological Seminary, she was heavily involved in the actual writing based on consultation with Sun Myung Moon and others.

Edwards, Jonathan. 1754. *Freedom of the Will.* Mineola, NY: Dover Publications, Inc. (2012).

Edwards, Jonathan. 1765. *Two Dissertations: I. Concerning the End for Which God Created the World; II. The Nature of True Virtue.* Widely available online. Originally begun in 1750 and published posthumously.

Edwards, Jonathan. 1829. *A Narrative of the Revival of Religion in New England; with Thoughts on That Revival.* Glasgow: William Collins. Reprinted on demand from the Harvard Book Store through Google Books. The first was published in 1737. More often found under the title "A Faithful Narrative". *Thoughts on the Revival of Religion in New England* was first published in 1742.

Edwards, Jonathan. 1999. *Religious Affections.* Abridged and updated by Ellyn Sanna. Part of The Essential Christian Library series. Uhrichsville, Ohio: Barbour Publishing. Originally published in 1746 under the title "A Treatise Concerning Religious Affections."

Edwards, Jonathan. 2004. *Praying Together for True Revival.* Edited by T. M. Moore. Phillipsburg, NJ: P&R Publishing Company. Usually published under the title "An Humble Attempt." Originally published in 1747 under the title "An Humble Attempt to Promote Explicit Agreement and Visible Union of God's People in Extraordinary Prayer for the Revival of Religion and the Advancement of Christ's Kingdom on Earth, Pursuant to Scripture Promises and Prophecies Concerning the Last Time."

Jonathan Edwards. 1741. *Sinners in the Hands of an Angry God.* Sermon originally delivered to Edwards own congregation in Northampton, Massachusetts. Edwards preached it a second time to the congregation in Enfield, Massachusetts on July 8, 1741. It is widely available in both written and audio versions.

Fackenheim, Emil L. 1982. *To Mend the World.* N.Y.: Schocken Books.

Freud, Sigmund. 1919. *Totem and Taboo.* A.A. Brill translator. N.Y.: Moffat, Yard and Company.

Fujimura, Makoto. 2017. *Culture Care, Reconnecting with Beauty for Our Common Life.* Downers Grove, IL: IVP Books (InterVarsity Press).

Gragg, Alan. 1973. *Charles Hartshorne.* Part of the series: *Makers of the Modern Theological Mind.* Edited by Bob E. Patterson. Peabody, MA: Hendrickson Publishers, Inc.

H-N

Hall, Christopher A. 2002. *Learning Theology With The Church Fathers.* Downers Grove, IL: InterVarsity Press.

Hebblethwaite, Peter. 1977. *The Christian-Marxist Dialogue: Beginnings, Present Status, and Beyond.* NY: Paulist Press.

Hong, Nansook. 1998. *In The Shadow Of The Moons: My Life In The Reverend Sun Myung Moon's Family.* Boston, New York, Toronto & London : Little, Brown & Co.

Hunter, George G. III. 2000. *The Celtic Way of Evangelism, How Christianity Can Reach the West... Again.* Nashville, TN: Abingdon Press.

Hunter, James Davison. 1991. *Culture Wars, The Struggle to Define America. Making sense of the battles over family, art education, law, and politics.* Nashville, TN: Basic Books.

Jacobs, Alan. 2017. *How to Think: A Survival Guide for a World at Odds.* New York: Currency, Crown Publishing Group.

Jones, E. Stanley. 1995. *The Unshakable Kingdom and the Unchanging Person.* Bellingham, WA: McNett Press. Reprinted by permission from Abingdon Press. ©1976.

Katz, Steven T. 1983. *Post-Holocaust Dialogues.* N.Y. & London: New York University Press.

Kaufmann, Frank. Quoted in "Blessing ceremony of the Unification Church." *Wikipedia.* Accessed: April 15,2019. https://en.wikipedia.org/wiki/Blessing_ceremony_of_the_Unification_Church

Lindgren, Caleb and Morgan Lee. 2018. "Our Favorite Heresies of 2018: Experts Weigh In," *CT Magazine,* October 26. Accessed: February 9, 2019. https://www.christianitytoday.com/news/2018/october/evangelicals-favorite-heresies-ligonier-theology-survey.html.

Luther, Martin. 1976. *The Bondage of the Will.* Translated by Henry Cole (1823). Grand Rapids, MI: Baker Book House.

Martin, Brian. 2004. "The Richardson dismissal as an academic boomerang" in *Workplace Mobbing in Academe: Reports from Twenty Universities.* Kenneth Westhues editor. Queenston, Ontario: Edwin Mellen Press. Available online March 13, 2019: https://www.bmartin.cc/pubs/04Westhues.html.

McDermott, Gerald R., editor. 2009. *Understanding Jonathan Edwards, An Introduction to America's Theologian.* NY:Oxford University Press.

McLuhan, Marshall. 1964. *Understanding Media: The Extensions of Man.* N.Y.: Signet Books.

Metaxas, Eric. 2010. *Bonhoeffer: Pastor, Martyr, Prophet, Spy.* Nashville, TN: Thomas Nelson, Inc.

Meyer, F.B. 1914. *Through the Bible Day by Day: A Devotional Commentary.* In the public domain. Widely available online and included in most Bible study software.

Niebuhr, H. Richard. 1959. *The Kingdom of God in America.* NY: Harper Torchbooks.

R-Z

Richardson, Herbert W. 1967. *Toward An American Theology.* New York, Evanston, and London: Harper & Row, Publishers.

Richardson, Herbert W., editor. 1981. *Ten Theologians Respond to the Unification Church.* New York: The Rose of Sharon Press, Inc.

Rubenstein, Richard L. 1966. *After Auschwitz: Radical Theology and Contemporary Judaism.* N.Y.: The Bobbs-Merrill Company.

Sontag, Frederick. 1977. *Sun Myung Moon and the Unification Church.* Nashville, TN: Abingdon Press.

Sontag, Frederick. 1978. "Being and Freedom: The Metaphysics of Freedom" in Process Studies, pp. 180-185, Vol. 8, Number 3, Fall, 1978. Claremont, CA: Center for Process Studies. Accessed online March 13, 2019: https://www.religion-online.org/article/being-and-freedom-the-metaphysics-of-freedom/ .

Stein, Ben, with Kevin Miller and Walt Ruloff. 2008. *Expelled: No Intelligence Allowed.* Premise Media Corporation and Rampant Films. Distributed in the US by Rocky Mountain Pictures. Available on DVD.

Sterns, Ken. 2017. *Republican Like Me: How I Left the Liberal Bubble and Learned to Love the Right.* NYC: HarperCollins Publishers. Kindle edition.

Tillich, Paul. 1952. *The Courage To Be.* New Haven, CT: Yale University Press.

Tillich, Paul. 1955. *The New Being.* NY: Charles Schribner's Sons.

Tracy, Patricia J. 1979. *Jonathan Edwards Pastor: Religion and Society in Eighteenth-Century Northampton.* New York: Hill and Wang.

Weber, Jeremy. 2018. "Pew: Why Americans Go to Church or Stay Home," *CT Magazine,* August 1. Accessed January 18, 2019. https://www.christianitytoday.com/news/2018/july/church-attendance-top-reasons-go-or-stay-home-pew.html.

Printed in the United States
By Bookmasters